Hidden Lessons

Hidden Lessons

Growing Up on the Frontline of Teaching

MEHREEN BAIG

HODDER*studio*

First published in Great Britain in 2021 by Hodder Studio
An Hachette UK company

1

Copyright © Mehreen Baig 2021

Epigraph on page v, from "The Rose That Grew from Concrete" used with permission from Amaru Entertainment, Inc.

A CIP catalogue record for this title is available from the British Library

Hardback ISBN 9781529383034
eBook ISBN 9781529383041

Typeset in Bembo MT by Hewer Text UK Ltd, Edinburgh
Printed and bound in Great Britain by Clays Ltd, Elcograf S.p.A.

Hodder & Stoughton policy is to use papers that are natural, renewable and recyclable products and made from wood grown in sustainable forests. The logging and manufacturing processes are expected to conform to the environmental regulations of the country of origin.

Hodder & Stoughton Ltd
Carmelite House
50 Victoria Embankment
London EC4Y 0DZ

www.hodder-studio.com

*'Long live the rose that grew from concrete
when no one else even cared!'*
Tupac Shakur

To my precious niece and nephew,
Amelia and Zach

I can write a whole book,
but I can't put into words
how much I love you.

Contents

Foreword

The most critical thing to say, before you read any further, is that this book is not a true story. When I was writing this book, I wanted to stay true to my authentic experiences as a teacher, but my priority had to be to protect the identity of my school, my colleagues and, most importantly, my students and their families. Therefore, the events and characters you read in this book have been fictionalised and are amalgamations of things I saw and people I knew. The names, dates, titles and stories are not real, but are based on and have been inspired by my real-life experiences and the experiences of my family and friends. Even Mr Thorne and Mr Wilson – two of the many heroes of this book – are inspired by real people, but have been heavily adapted using my overactive imagination and love for Mr Darcy.

It is also important to say that this book does not highlight every teacher's experience, every young person's experience, every working-class person's experience, every Muslim's experience, or every British Pakistani's experiences. This is just my story. It's what I saw, my life, my personal views, my perspective. With over 500,000 teachers currently working in the United Kingdom, no doubt our experiences will differ dramatically, but I hope some of this will ring true, or at least seem a little familiar.

I started teaching straight out of university and had no real idea what I was getting myself into. Like most twenty-something-year-olds, I thought I knew everything, when really I knew very little. Teaching in that school, back on the street where I had grown up, was a dream, and writing this book has been the most cathartic experience because it made me recall all the memories that were quietly resting somewhere in the corners of my mind and gave me the joy of reliving them.

I'm sure all jobs change you, but nothing prepares you for life like teaching. Schools are all of life, a strange ecosystem with hierarchies, challenges and unique characters. Each of those elements teaches you something that you can take into the 'real' world. I'm not saying I have all the answers – because trust me, I'm still figuring life out every day – but every year I spent in the classroom, I learned something fundamental about myself or society.

These stories provide just a small window into the breathtaking perseverance, strength of character, resilience and courage I witnessed during my time as a teacher. It would be impossible to encapsulate each child and each teacher I met in ten chapters – so the ones you will read about here represent a very small proportion and serve as a microcosm for some of the wider issues we see in Britain today.

When Twitter and the mainstream media erupt with their usual anti-teacher headlines, I sometimes get heated in my responses because I have witnessed first-hand how much my colleagues and other teachers around the country give to their job and the kids. They do it because they believe in the young people. They look at your children and see the future hairdresser, architect, footballer, doctor, gymnast, rapper, lawyer, actor, engineer and designer. They root for them, build them up physically, socially, morally, ethically – and of course educate them. Your children spend more time at school than they do at home, and when they find that teacher who speaks to them, that magic is indescribable.

I hope that this book will take you into the whirlwind that is teaching so that you can see the utter brilliance of the profession, but also gain some degree of insight into the challenges that the job really entails. This book isn't an exhaustive look at the school system, a polemic about its failings, or a love story. It's not my memoir (we'll get to that, one day), but it's a collection of the important lessons that have stuck with me.

So, as you enter my mind palace, and sieve through my wonderful memories, if there is one teacher, or one student whose story ends up staying with you, then I would feel like I had won a gold star.

I will always speak out for the teaching profession and I will always stand up for young people. In some of my toughest times, it was my students who kept me going – their positivity, their invincible spirit, and their ability to crack tension with just one outrageous comment.

This book is a tribute to each and every one of them.

Prologue

In 2018, I left teaching for television. The decision to swap my red pen for a blue tick wasn't easy – but stress-induced thrush helps make a hard choice simpler. In my leaving speech, I promised the staff and students I would never forget them and, with a quivering bottom lip, shared Googled motivational quotes on being brave and following your dreams. During that one minute, I questioned whether I was doing the right thing about a million times. But, in the words of Macbeth, I had 'done the deed': my resignation had been accepted and I had no choice but to push back the worries and try to visualise my future celebrity self, living a life of hot yoga and personal stylists. Manifesting and all that.

Two years later, I was still living in my childhood bedroom, spending evenings online shopping and getting told off by my mum for coming home too late every Friday night. I did like my new job, and enjoyed being surrounded by quirky and creative people, working in different settings every day. I told myself it was a good thing to be out of my comfort zone, that I would soon get used to speaking to a camera, rather than a human. The funny thing was that whilst I was in awe of the brave new world I was immersed in, it was my old life as a teacher that intrigued people. It became my party trick at networking events – when people first met me, they brushed me off as 'an influencer' – then I would casually mention that I used to be a teacher and suddenly they were fascinated. The more details I provided, the more respect I got. What subject? What age group? Which area? By the time I dropped 'Tottenham', they were eating out of my hands.

When you're a teacher, it's easy to forget that, for most people, school is a distant memory of exam stress, detentions and PE. They all want to know what it's like from the other side and have that window into the classroom. So when the opportunity came along to film a project at my old school and teach a class on camera, I jumped at it. I was still adjusting to television, but I knew teaching inside out.

But in the weeks building up to the recording, I started getting those recurring nightmares again where I entered a classroom and began to teach, only to realise I was naked. It was like the end-of-summer-holiday dread but on steroids. Irrational anxiety and a barrage of questions infiltrated my mind: how would I get the students to settle down? What if they didn't listen to me? What would I do if they answered back? I utilised my time in the shower by replaying a range of potentially humiliating scenarios and practised how I would deal with them.

On the morning of the shoot, my anxiety was through the roof. I made that exact journey into school I'd done thousands of times from my parents' house. I walked through the same gates, dodging shouting children and pulling down the back of my skirt like I'd done almost every morning in my twenties. I entered the same building in which I'd once spent more hours than my own home, and it all felt exactly the same but totally different. Hardly anything had changed, from the same slightly unloved plants to the same messages on the noticeboards. But I was conscious of the production team following at my heels, and seeing the curious expressions all around me, I realised I didn't belong here anymore. The familiar sound of students laughing and teachers shouting floated through the air, but instead of providing me with any comfort, it only added to my dread. In three years, I'd moved from an insider to a visitor, uneasy in the commotion of the corridor.

I tried to distract myself by talking the team through some of the displays, and pointing out where my old classroom used to be. But the entire time, my mind was frantically trying to work out how I'd teach a class when I'd forgotten the first thing about teaching. I searched for the exits when my ears picked up on something that I knew didn't sound quite right. I can't explain what it was that made me pause – no one else seemed to notice anything unusual – but my gut told me that something was wrong.

Slowing down, I edged closer towards the offending classroom, just to ensure that my concerns were valid and I wasn't hallucinating from the insomnia of the night before – but one peek through the window and my fears were confirmed.

I pushed open the classroom door and was stunned by the scene unfolding in front of me. It was like a Renaissance painting – a full tableau of bad behaviour spreading from one side of the classroom to the other. At the far end, almost sheltering behind a desk, was a teacher who I didn't recognise – clearly new, from the deer in the headlights look on her face. A wrestling match was taking place a metre away from her. At a glance, it was hard to work out how many bodies were stuck together to form this mass of legs and arms, but I guessed at least five. To complete the picture, taking up the rest of the room, were close to thirty students standing on tables, some cheering, others filming, and a couple of them just using the opportunity to jump from table to table in a heated round of The Floor is Lava.

A voice boomed across the room.

'What on earth do you think you're doing? Get into your seats AT ONCE!'

My voice.

For a moment, I wondered whether that had done the trick or if I would be treated like a supply teacher with no real authority. They didn't recognise me – I'd left before their year started – and the students seemed equally unsure about their next move. But they could smell that I wasn't a novice and wasn't to be messed with, in the way that teenagers always can. The air was still. I decided to step it up a gear and started scanning the room with sudden and vigorous deliberate head movements, periodically landing and then lingering on one randomly selected poor soul, as if I were looking for the chief culprit. After a few seconds of confusion and hesitation, the crowd began to slowly shift and disperse.

I counted to ten before moving on to my next trick, which I call The Guinea Pig. I picked a student whose only crime was moving slowly and, feigning sarcastic surprise (always more disconcerting than the shouting), said, 'Darling – didn't you hear what I just said?' And then – BAM! – I hit the boy next to him with a snappy, 'What's that smile on your face about? Did I say something funny?' Like puppets, the class settled into their seats, knowing it was best to avoid any accidental eye contact with this unstable bitch.

8

Within the next sixty seconds, I had delegated a responsible-looking student to go and get the behaviour mentor, and then sent a second student after her, just in case; I had lectured the students on the gravity of the situation, highlighted the danger they had put everyone in, foreshadowed potential consequences, even throwing in a bit of legal jargon for emphasis, and had everyone writing witness statements in silence.

By now, their teacher had sunk into her chair with her hands in her lap and a look of resignation on her face. I knew exactly how she felt. Utter relief that she was no longer in the middle of a storm, a sense of awe that it was possible to impose some control on children in that state, embarrassment at the thought she'd never be able to, and anxiety that the children wouldn't forget that someone else had to swoop in. I knew how she felt because I had been her just ten years before.

I caught her eye and we smiled at each other. I wish I could have said 'It gets better', or 'Next time someone throws a punch, take that whiteboard eraser and slam it down on the table so hard it shocks everyone into submission'. I knew my coming in might have undermined her authority, and she'd have to work even harder to establish it. But that commanding presence wasn't something that could be learned by listening to a lecture or reading a book; she would figure it out for herself in the series of unfortunate events that took place in the classroom. Working out how to do that had taken me many stressful and chaotic months.

Once the behaviour mentor arrived, I explained the situation to him in detail, and with a final apology to the poor classroom teacher for the disappointing behaviour of our students, turned around and swished out of the classroom.

The film crew were in utter shock. I don't blame them – what they had witnessed was nothing short of possession, where my voice, my posture, my entire being had completely transformed within seconds. I didn't say a word, and they followed me to the class I now had to teach. I knew I could do it.

I thought I'd forgotten what I'd learned, but the truth is, you never really stop being a teacher. Just like riding a bike, once you have those skills, you never lose them. Sensing the danger, using the eyes at the back of my head, reacting quickly, considering all possible outcomes, it all came back. Muscle memory.

I couldn't tell you when exactly over the last ten years I had acquired these tools, and when exactly the transform-ation from mere mortal to teacher took place. I have no idea when I stopped being that helpless teacher at the front of the class and developed the skills, the empathy, maturity and knowledge necessary to be able to deal with any situation. I've taught *The Great Gatsby* so many times I could recite it – and just like Nick Carraway, my journey changed me from an inexperienced newbie to a 'guide, a pathfinder, counsel-lor, security guard, a nurse and an educator . . .' Well, he didn't exactly say that, but you get my drift.

It's weird – in one way, teaching felt like the most suffo-cating and rigid profession, where every hour of every day of every week had been timetabled. Utterly inflexible holi-day dates had been scheduled a year in advance and I had exactly fifteen minutes at 10.55 a.m. to piss – if I was lucky. Yet at the same time, I felt like I was on a rollercoaster, full of unimaginable highs and even more traumatic lows. It was fast paced and thrilling, sometimes terrifying, and often I felt like I was hanging on for dear life.

Once I left the classroom and had the time to process and reflect, only then did I appreciate how unpredictable teaching really is. There are so many variables beyond your control. You can spend the whole night planning the most innovative lessons, but when you enter the school gates that morning, you have no idea what is going to kick off. Are you going to change someone's life today? Are you going to risk your own?

But despite the challenges and more than anything, it was a privilege to watch my students grow up over the years and witness their journey first-hand from childhood to adulthood. And I guess, somewhere along the way, in the hours I spent in my classroom, I grew up too.

A decade provided me with a crash course in learning about myself, as well as the world around me; I grew up behind those gates, and as I walked out of them for the last time, everything looked different.

It's only now when I look back that I truly understand the hidden lessons those ten years taught me.

I

Sometimes You Just Have to Act the Part

When I first started teaching, I thought I would save the world. You know the image, Robin Williams-style, children standing on tables in front of me reciting poetry in adoration. I was sure it would be that easy; I'd be centre stage, imparting wisdom to an eager audience desperate to learn. Every day would be a dreamy haze of inspiration and education. Lol.

It took me a while to figure out what I actually wanted to do with my life. Up until the age of seventeen, I thought I was going to be a doctor – partly because I was a super-high achiever at school and partly because I'm Pakistani and my occupation had been determined along with my gender at birth. But that plan didn't quite work out. My brother discovered he was very sick during my time at college and I simultaneously discovered a hugely distracting species called boys. The lethal combination of the two meant I missed my medicine offer in a colossal fuck-up of an A-level results day. I vividly recall sitting cross-legged on the pavement outside my college, bawling my eyes out, wishing I had prepared more thoroughly for my exams. I regretted all the times I had truanted and procrastinated, and promised myself that I would be more focused in the future.

So, I went through Clearing and eventually ended up taking English at university. Which was fine . . . except I still didn't have any real purpose or plan for the future. I once applied to a graduate scheme to become an Area Manager of a popular supermarket chain. It was random, but the pay and the perks seemed like a dream come true and on my way to the location, I even found a crisp £50 note under a car, so I thought Lady Luck was on my side. When I arrived for the interview, there were fifteen other candidates sitting around a large table and I took my place amongst them. We were asked to introduce ourselves, one by one, stating our names and sharing one interesting fact about ourselves. Easy, I thought. I quickly jotted down a couple of notes about what my interesting fact could be – there were so many to choose from. English is actually my second language, I once auditioned for *X Factor*, I got nine A*s at GCSE . . . Hmm, that one may seem a bit braggy, I thought, so I put a question mark next to it.

They started at the opposite end of the table, and I smiled encouragingly at the first person to speak. He didn't meet my eye. 'Um, hi everyone,' he didn't smile, the poor thing. 'My name is Dom, and last year, I climbed Mount Kilimanjaro, raising £3 million for British Red Cross.' I stared at him incredulously, and he stared right back at me, almost as if he was saying, 'Take that!' I looked away quickly, and focused on the next person who was about to speak.

'Hi everyone,' a girl with shiny auburn hair and freckles began to speak. 'My name is Jessica, and last year, I completed the passage through the land of fire and ice and raised £3.5 million for the Donkey Sanctuary.' I stared at her blankly.

Was that a metaphor? I looked around frantically at everyone else to see whether they were in on the joke, but they were giving nods of approval. Was this genuinely a thing? Was this a normal part of British life that I had just completely missed out on? One by one, each person in the circle stated their interesting fact, some of them had jumped out of planes, whilst others had shagged on the moon – all in the name of charity – and by the time it was my turn, my mind was blank and I had no idea what on earth I could say that would even vaguely compare to these extraordinary feats.

'Hi . . . my name is Mehreen,' I paused, 'like . . . a submarine,' I giggled awkwardly, and no one's mouth moved even a millimetre, not even in pity, so I continued, 'Um . . . and my interesting fact is that I, er, well, just this morning, I was on my way here, when I found a fifty-pound note under a car tyre.' There was silence. 'And now, I will be donating it to Children in Need.' I didn't stay for the second round.

After that utterly mortifying experience, I was back to square one. My friends at university didn't seem too bothered about their own future plans. It felt like most of the students were only there to have fun rather than study, and for many of them, 'education' was funded by the Bank of Mummy and Daddy, but I didn't have that luxury. I began tutoring students a few years younger than me for some extra money. There's nothing like explaining Chaucer to a hungover nineteen-year-old to whet one's appetite for teaching. I got a strange satisfaction from watching someone get to grips with a text and, without ever meaning to, I was set on a path. Coffee-shop sessions with the odd student developed into teaching at a tuition centre, which turned into volunteering at my sister's school during the holidays. It still took a good couple of years for the penny to finally drop and I realised that this was something I was genuinely really good at. I enjoyed educating young people – not just academically, but socially and emotionally. It seemed I had finally found my purpose.

The decision to teach at a secondary school was pretty simple. People say teenagers are difficult, but it's adults that I really struggle with. Teenagers are honest: they say how they feel, for better or for worse, and there are no mind games involved. If they like you, they buy you a 'Best Teacher' mug and if they hate you, they throw a chair at you. They're quite simple, really. Bad behaviour wasn't something I was ever concerned about – I was born in Hackney and raised in a council estate in Tottenham that even the police didn't enter. These kids couldn't scare me. I had seen real life and I was prepared.

As some of my rich friends prepared to explore their spirituality in India on gap years, I got ready for my teacher training. For anyone who doesn't know what that entails, I hope you enjoy your marking-free life and discounted holidays in January. Teacher training is exactly what it sounds like: an immersive year of learning the craft, typically involving a lot of time observing and teaching in school, as well as all the un-fun parts of university – long, tedious, mundane essays about nothing. You watch lessons in apprehensive wonder, and learn the ropes from seasoned pros. It's intense, exhaustive and eye-opening, just like teaching. The year before me, due to a teacher shortage, the cohort were offered a £6,000 bursary for an English PGCE and the year after, the lucky bastards were offered £9,000. It was just my good fortune that in 2011, the government cut the funding and I was given the whopping figure of £0. And no, that's not a typo. It gives you some idea of my luck. Further unpaid study meant that my student loan would substantially increase, but still that didn't put me off. I was twenty-one, straight out of university and I was ready to make my mark on the world.

Or so I thought.

During the first half of my training course, I was assigned a placement school and partnered with an older teacher, Ms Abbot. I'd sit at the back of all her lessons, barely distinguishable from her students. The school looked very much like the one I'd left only a few years before – grey, nondescript, loud and heaving with children. But nothing quite prepares you for walking in as one of the adults in the room, and I kept waiting to be told off for not wearing uniform.

If I'm completely honest, the whole teaching thing looked quite easy from where I was sitting; I watched her, day in and day out, from the comfort of the invisible corner of the classroom, judging her every move and profusely making notes of any 'good and bad practice' she demonstrated. Ms Abbot was the kind of teacher who had a scary reputation amongst the students (and some of the staff), but once you got to know her you discovered she was brimming with sarcastic wit. The fact that the students didn't always understand her jokes led me to believe that she cracked them for her own entertainment, rather than anyone else's.

In those first few weeks, I took the fact she didn't really smile, and her no-nonsense approach with her class, to mean she was a bad teacher who didn't know how to relate to the kids. Sometimes, when she told off a student for inappropriate banter, I would catch their eye and give them a sympathetic 'Well, *I* thought it was funny, she is *so* unreasonable' kind of look. I often observed her lessons and thought about how I would handle certain situations differently – how I would handle them *so* much better.

Considering what a patronising and deluded arsehole I was, Ms Abbot was really good to me. She would only give me four books to mark a day, and let me sneak out early on Fridays, when she had no afternoon lessons. One day after school, when we were slogging through reams of coursework and filing them into piles of 'completed', 'needs catch-up sessions' and 'needs teacher to rewrite entirely', I asked her why she always seemed so serious, to which she simply replied, 'Teachers shouldn't smile until Christmas, Miss Baig.'

I wasn't sure what she meant and didn't bother to ask either. I looked at Ms Abbot and saw a teacher who wasn't acting like the inspirational leader I wanted to be. I dismissed her strategy, without considering that her experience meant that she knew what she was talking about.

In Ms Abbot's class, I saw very little bad behaviour and witnessed only low-level disruption, but at the end of term, things went from 0 to 100 in a matter of moments. The Year 11 class was in the middle of an assessment when an outrageously tall boy asked Ms Abbot if he could go to the toilet. She declined his request in her usual sardonic manner, reminding him that there wasn't long to go until break-time, before turning back to her computer screen. The rest of the scene is embedded within my memory in slow motion: the boy got out of his seat and made his way through the desks to the back of the classroom, where all the coursework was carefully laid out. He turned and took one final, meaningful look back at Ms Abbot, pulled out his penis, and pissed all over it.

It was dreadful. Completely dreadful. Culturally, I had grown up with an elevated status of the teacher cemented in my mind – and answering back, or disrespecting this fountain of all knowledge, was never an option. As I watched this dirty 'baptism' of the coursework, I realised my own baptism of fire had arrived. Like the glassy-eyed beginner I was, I sat in a state of rigid shock as the class erupted around me. The girls made retching noises, the boys laughed and shouted, and everyone lurched backwards to avoid any direct hits. Ms Abbot watched quietly until silence descended and every child was looking at the terrifying expression on her face. Quietly, she asked the rest of the class to wait outside, signalled for me to stay with her and took out her mobile phone to call for some assistance. As they all filed out, I looked between Ms Abbot and the boy, disgusted by the student I'd so identified with only moments before.

The boy stood in a puddle of his urine, in a predicament of his own. He had emptied his bladder without considering the aftermath of his actions, and now seemed to be recognising for the first time that this might not have been the best idea he ever had. Ms Abbot kept her eyes firmly down and didn't say a word. This obviously wasn't their first rodeo. The boy knew he'd crossed a line, and Ms Abbot knew it too. The awkward silence was interrupted only when the cleaner arrived, complete with paper towels and a mop, and the Head of Year followed shortly behind. He marched the boy out of the classroom – who, by this point, was shitting himself – excuse the pun. As the rest of the class were relocated, I was sent to the staffroom to recover whilst Ms Abbot was made to act as though nothing had ever happened.

In her last look to me, I could see all the years of similar behaviour, all the instances of complete disrespect. Her sarcasm and frustration suddenly made sense and, in that moment, I knew that I was not a student any more but not quite a teacher yet, either. I was tentatively balancing on the brink of both parts.

I got through the rest of the year without any major drama. My second placement was at a grammar school in a wealthy area, where students stood up when the teachers entered the classroom and everyone was high achieving, and I personally thought it was boring as hell. It was like the Canary Wharf of schools – and for those of you who haven't been to Canary Wharf at the weekend, it may be the heaving heart of finance, but it is utterly soulless. Whether or not it was my own insecurities shining through, I could never shake the feeling that both the students and teachers could tell that I just didn't fit in, and the parents seemed perturbed that a British-Pakistani, working-class girl was teaching their children English. So, when I started looking for jobs, I took it as a clear sign from God that there was an English-teacher vacancy in my hometown of Tottenham.

My father dropped me off on the morning of the interview, and we saw the headteacher waiting for all the candidates outside the school gates. To my utter mortification, as I got out of the car, my dad wound down the window of his banger and shouted, 'You've got the job, darl! The job is yours! You're a star!' And with that, he performed his trademark twelve-point turn and drove away. It was like the first day of school all over again.

The minute I stepped into that building, I knew it was the place for me. I felt it in my bones. The other candidates and I followed the headteacher down the corridor towards his office, and each classroom radiated with an indescribable buzz. Along the way, students ran ahead to hold open the door for us and beamed in excitement as we walked through.

Some wished us luck as they passed with an encouraging wink. The kids were confident, charming, polite, and I desperately wanted to be a part of this world. It was an energy like I had never witnessed in any school before, as if the whole thing had been carefully choreographed for me.

The interview was spread across the day in three different stages: there was a student panel (a bit like speed dating, though less pressure), an observed lesson and, finally, an interview with the head and other members of senior leadership. It was gruelling – but there was no way I was going to let anyone else take this job from me. My interview was the last of the day, so at 5.50 p.m., I topped up my lip gloss for some additional boss-babe energy and strode into the headteacher's office, ready to show them what I'm all about.

My memory of the actual interview is a bit of a blur, though I can recall regurgitating some key phrases that my siblings had drilled into me the night before. I repeated jargon that I didn't truly understand – 'SEN', 'differentiation', 'pupil premium' – like teacher's Tourette's. As the interview came to a close, I was packing my folder away when it suddenly dawned on me that these were the last few seconds I had to show this panel how passionately I wanted this job. My mind went to the kids I'd passed in the corridor, and with sudden inspiration, I stopped mid-action, looked up and said, 'I just want to say that I grew up on these streets, went to the primary school next door, and would love the opportunity to be able to help the students who are growing up just like me.' They smiled. Confidence spread through me like wildfire. And before I knew it, the following words came tumbling out of my mouth: 'I just want to add that people think you can't be both pretty and clever but I just want to prove that you can.' I have no idea where that came from and I still haven't lived it down with my friends. It's like something from *Legally Blonde* that I'd dug up and decided was appropriate for the beleaguered and bewildered secondary school headteacher in front of me. And with that grand ending, I picked up my folder, thanked them for their time, and sashayed out of the room.

I don't know how or why I got the job, but they chose to overlook the narcissism and offered me the role. And a couple of months later, I was set to embark on my new adventure, ready to change young people's lives.

But you see, the slight issue with changing young people's lives is that it's a very difficult task when you're a young person yourself.

On 2 September 2012, a mild autumnal morning, I woke up at 5.15 a.m. I was in my childhood bedroom, and opened the same cupboard that used to hold my school uniform. All my old clothes had been pushed to the back. Hanging in front of me, there was a row of new outfits I had spent the summer buying and putting together – skirts and blouses in an array of colours, and a couple of polo necks for the days I wanted to look extra smart. I picked out a light blue silky shirt (that was only £10 from Bardo but looked really posh) and a multicoloured pencil skirt and carefully placed my outfit on my bed, before heading to the shower. I had given myself plenty of time to get ready, and I sat in front of my mirror, backcombing my hair before adding hair extensions. I carefully applied a face full of make-up – extra eyeliner to disguise the fact that I hadn't slept very well – and after putting on a pair of ridiculously high heels, I stood for several minutes staring at myself in the mirror. I felt like a grown-up.

Downstairs, Mum was preparing my breakfast for my big day – first day at school. As I tottered down the stairs and into the kitchen, she turned and looked at me with a quizzical expression.

'Do I look OK?' I asked her, eyes wide in anticipation.

'You look beautiful,' she replied after a second's hesitation, and placed a full Pakistani breakfast on the table in front of me.

I sat down to eat it but suddenly wasn't feeling very hungry. Mum was pacing around the kitchen, spouting out last-minute advice: 'Don't get nervous. Be confident. Don't panic. Make friends.' I could sense she was just as nervous as me. I pretended to eat in silence, pushing my food around my plate for what seemed like a realistic amount of time, and just as I finished my meal, my father came out of the bathroom, ready to drop me at the tube station. He stopped as he caught sight of me.

'Are you going to work or a fashion show?' he asked.

I looked at Mum and rolled my eyes, and she shook her head in a 'Don't mind him' kind of way. He so didn't get it.

Only, he did get it, and he was right. By the time I was standing on the other side of my desk watching thirty-two kids pour into the classroom, I felt ridiculous. My classroom was quite small and plain, but luckily I was going to be in there for all my lessons, so I wouldn't have to walk around the school building like in my training school, which was great because my feet were aching already. When I saw my timetable in the morning after staff briefing, I was quite surprised at how packed it looked. I had been given a Year 7 class, a Year 8 class, two Year 10 classes and a Year 11 class, and each class would see me for four lessons per week. I tried to colour in my 'free periods' boxes, but there were hardly any to colour. Overwhelmed with all of the information I had been given, I didn't even get a chance to really think about my first lesson, so by the time the bell rang, I felt terrified. My clothes clung to my sweaty body like a *Strictly Come Dancing* costume and I could sense their sceptical eyes scrutinising me from head to toe, unsure of what to make of this stranger. Waking up at 5 a.m. to get ready had seemed like a good idea at the time, but now I felt I had overcompensated to adopt the persona of a 'proper' teacher.

Luckily, my first class was a Year 7 one, which meant that the eleven-year-olds on their first day of secondary school didn't know much better than I did. They were quiet and awkward as they came in and then found a place behind one of the seats and stared at me expectantly.

I was more terrified than I had ever been before. I stepped further behind my desk to hide legs that were visibly shaking, but my voice still betrayed my nerves as I tried to take the students through the 'Get to know me!' starter. They were great – whether they saw through me or not, they obediently listened to my classroom rules of 'no swearing, no eating', etc. and engaged in the activity. As they shared two truths and a lie with each other, I also had my first proper opportunity to take a register of the students. I got through the first few names, and they answered with differing variations of 'Here, Miss' and 'Present, Miss'. But when I got to the fifth name on the list, Ceylan, I stumbled a little bit.

'Um . . . *See* . . . *Say* . . .' I knew how annoying it was when people pronounced my name incorrectly. My whole life, teachers called me 'Munir' and baristas wrote 'Mary' on my cup, and I really wanted to get it right for my own students. 'Seelan?' I attempted again, and scanned the room for the owner of the name. A couple of the students giggled.

'Here, Miss.' A small, quiet girl sitting in the corner smiled shyly at me. I smiled back and was about to continue when another student put her hand up, wobbling around in her seat like she was about to burst.

'Miss!' she hissed. 'Miss!'

'Yes?' I asked.

'You said her name wrong. It's Jay-lan.'

I looked back over to Ceylan, and she looked embarrassed by the attention.

'Oh, I'm so sorry, sweetheart,' I said, horrified, 'I'll remember that for next time.' And then I turned back to the girl who had corrected me. 'Thank you for telling me.'

'That's all right, Miss. My name's Angel. You can see why.' She grinned and posed theatrically whilst the class fell about into giggles. I immediately liked them.

For the second half of the lesson, I asked the class to write me a short letter, introducing themselves to me and telling me a bit more about their likes and dislikes. I typed out the date, title and some instructions onto the board and, after a bit of excited chatter and shuffling around, they eventually settled down and started to write. As I was about to enjoy my first pause of the lesson, a hand shot up again, and I jolted up, wondering what on earth I had done wrong this time.

'Miss! Miss!' There was the same sense of urgency, but this time the voice belonged to a boy who was wearing glasses that were far too big for his face and a jumper that was stretched over his plump body. His name was Daniel.

'Yes, darling?' I said.

'Is that the date?' he said, face scrunched up in confusion, pointing his finger at my screen. *Nah, it is my phone number,* I thought to myself, but to him I said, 'Yes, it is.' He nodded earnestly and turned back to his blank page.

Ten seconds later, his hand went up again. 'Do we underline?'

'Yes.'

Then, like a contagion, other hands started shooting up, asking me if they could 'write in blue pen' or, my personal favourite, if they were supposed to 'turn over the page when they got to the end'.

The incessant questioning continued until the hour was up, and with each one, I was reliving my earlier anxiety. I was constantly on edge, thinking any minute now one of them would realise I'm not a real teacher and call me out. Luckily they didn't, they played along, and we somehow got through the lesson.

Whilst the students made their way out of my class-room, I fiddled with some papers on my desk whilst trying to overhear the feedback being shared between them. Angel whispered, 'That was sick' to her friend, and little did she know that those three ungrammatical words were the only validation I needed to be able to face the rest of the day. As I collected their exercise books, the last book I added to my pile was Daniel's, which had 'YOUR NAME' copied onto the front where his own name should have been.

By 4 p.m., and after five consecutive lessons and a sand-wich at my desk, I was exhausted; in fact, I was utterly fucked. My feet had blisters, my eyes were sore and my voice had broken like a twelve-year-old boy's. I sat at my desk, head in my hands, and all I could think was . . . *I have to go in tomorrow.* So what did I do? What could I do but go home and prepare for the next day?

And that's what I did every evening for my first term. The only way I had the confidence to step in front of the students was by scripting my lessons, so I wrote out pages and pages of every single word I would say for every single hour of every single class the next day. I shit you not, I even wrote 'Hi, my name is Miss Baig. Please put your bags under the table.' Each moment was intricately planned. And for every day of the next term, I stuck the new scripts to my desk and basically read them out. That's how I survived my first few weeks.

As I got to know the students, I realised how much we had in common. I enjoyed hearing their weird and wonderful stories and often, it felt like we were in a study group, rather than in a lesson. I remember teaching *The Merchant of Venice* to my Year 9s, and reading the scene where Shylock discovers that his daughter, Jessica, has run away from home, taking a chest of her father's money with her. Some of the class were shocked by what Jessica had done, whilst the others empathised with a child who was living with an overbearing parent, and had no other option but to elope with the man she loved. Before long, we were in a full-blown discussion about strict parents and the responsibilities of children.

'Do children need rules?' I asked the class.

'Well, if your child's a girl, then yes,' Marvin shouted out with a grin.

Candice's hand shot straight up into the air. 'I don't agree. Marvin is definitely more in need of rules than me.' The class giggled. 'Anyway, the issue isn't that she ran away. It's the fact that she took her dad's money.'

In a mad moment of confidence, I deviated completely from my script and decided to start a debate.

'Right.' I took a quick seat at my computer and started transcribing as I spoke, 'I want everyone on the left-hand side to think of all the reasons why children should have the right to go against their parents, and you guys,' I said, turning to face the group on the right, 'need to argue why they don't. And when this timer runs out . . .' I quickly stuck a timer on the board, 'each group will present their ideas.'

It was like something had been unlocked. The students burst into excited discussions until it was time for feedback.

Lucas was first to put his hand up.

'Yeah, I think children should be able to say no to their parents because parents are not always right and sometimes they could be asking you to do something wrong, so you have to learn to say no.' He finished, evidently proud of himself.

A girl called Martyna hesitantly spoke next.

'I think even if you want to do something your parents disagree with, you should try to convince them first, and get their blessing, because they are your parents and worked hard to raise you. And they know what's best for you.' She paused, and looked at me for approval and I smiled. Martyna had only moved to the country from Spain a year ago, and was still getting to grips with the English language. To see her have the courage to speak in front of the whole class and the confidence to convey her point of view filled me with pride.

'Well, I believe that . . . you can't always listen to your parents because you only live once,' Marvin shouted out, without putting his hand up, which wasn't unusual for him.

'You only live once: that's the motto, YOLO!' The class burst into fits of laughter and started chanting, 'And we 'bout it every day, every day, every day,' whilst Marvin broke into a little dance, and I laughed along too as everyone settled back on task, writing out their personal response to Jessica's elopement. It was thrilling. No lesson plan, no script, and it was one of the best lessons I had ever had, with Drake and the Bard fitting together in perfect harmony.

In many ways, I probably felt more comfortable in the company of the students than the teachers. I had nothing to offer in the staffroom – I didn't have the knowledge or the confidence to participate in the heated and wide-ranging topical debates, where my colleagues were discussing whether or not Obama should be re-elected, the legitimacy of the monarchy in preparation of the Queen's Diamond Jubilee and the forthcoming Olympics. Looking around the tables, I was acutely aware that I had not yet formed any friendships with any of these people and had no idea what to say to them. I didn't care about mortgages and pensions, but in the classroom I felt like I could be myself. Being a young teacher meant my students and I watched the same TV shows and were following the same make-up trends. It also meant I understood them, and could connect with them on their level. I had a sense of what might be troubling them, because I wasn't so far from those troubles myself. I knew I had to strike that balance between being empathetic but also setting clear and firm boundaries. I also knew that I wasn't quite there yet.

By the time Christmas was round the corner, my life had very quickly become consumed by my new job; I had always suffered from insomnia, but now I would fall asleep from as much as a gentle tap on the bum like a baby. Where I could easily do all-nighters and go to lectures the next day just a year before, I was now barely able to keep my eyes open past sunset. I woke up at 5 a.m. to get dolled up and arrived at school at 7.30 a.m. to make sure my classroom was ready, resources were printed and photocopied, and the scripts were stuck to the desk for the day. From 8.30 a.m. onwards, I taught back-to-back lessons, bouncing and skipping around the room to provide the optimum service for my students. After school, I filled out spreadsheets, responded to emails that had stacked up during the day and ran into meetings, usually late because a member of my tutor group had lost her pencil case or best friend, or both, yet again. I was constantly switched on. Falling asleep on the tube journey home and missing my stop became a regular occurrence. Once home, I scoffed down some dinner, and spent the hours between 6 and 8 p.m. learning the next text I was about to teach in enough depth, planning lessons for the next day and marking work until eventually falling asleep on a pile of unmarked exercise books. I no longer possessed the time nor the energy to offer any more than a grunt for people once I left that building. Between all of this, it's no wonder all other personal relationships blurred into the background.

I'd been with my boyfriend for a few years and it was very much first-love territory. He was extroverted and outgoing, which, compared to my sheltered upbringing, made him seem extremely exciting. We met in a shisha bar – I know, it's hardly an Austen-esque romantic setting, but shisha bars are the twenty-first-century Asian equivalent of a Regency ballroom. He approached me with such confidence – charming me and making all my friends laugh – that it was quite difficult to resist. Not to make myself sound like a gold-digger, but let's just say that he was from quite a wealthy family, which meant I had gone from buying 'similar to as seen on TV' from Netto to receiving designer bags. My students saw him coming to pick me up in his fancy car, and I must confess, I was very quickly swept away by it all.

I used to sneak out of my house a few times a week or pretend I had late-night revision at university to spend time with him and we used to go to fancy places, sit in the VIP area and order more dishes than we could eat. Often, when we were out, girls would approach him, and act as though I didn't exist, throwing themselves all over him, and I stood at the side being the understanding and supportive girlfriend, admiring how comfortably he handled being the centre of attention. On the days that I couldn't escape without being caught by my parents, I would dutifully wait for his endless partying to finish and he would call me when he got home to tell me he was safe and say goodnight. Sometimes, I would set an alarm for 3 a.m., just in case I accidentally nodded off.

We were very serious: a couple of years into the relationship, he was the first boy to meet my family, and it was probably the biggest moment of my life. I spent hours getting ready and cleaning the house, telling Mum she had to take out the best dinner set and the new CorningWare glasses that had been sitting in a box waiting for a special occasion, so that we didn't look poor. He arrived outside my humble abode in his Ferrari, spent some time with my sister and my brother, eating and talking about football, and I busied myself around the kitchen, serving the food and being the perfect wifey. My father joined them about an hour in, waited for about sixty seconds, and then walked back into the living room. When my mum followed him, he quite simply said, 'Get that bastard out of my house.' But to be honest, it didn't matter what any of them thought, because I knew the real him: I knew how much fun we had, how protective and generous and caring he was. He was perfect for me, and we were both, quite simply, smitten.

But since starting teaching we'd begun arguing more and more. The arguments were mostly about the same thing: he just couldn't understand why I was so tired all the time when all I did was read from a textbook all day and I was never like this before and why didn't I dress up when I saw him lately and why couldn't I see him every day like I used to?

Trying to make my boyfriend happy, keep my friends close and manage my parents was like being a teenager all over again. Sometimes I almost forgot I wasn't one, and when you're only a few years older than your students it can be easy to forget they aren't your friends. One of the difficulties of being a young teacher is finding the balance between building positive relationships with students but ensuring they take you and your authority seriously, and that can be a really difficult balance to find. As work began to devour more hours of my life, I started to see my students as the only constant source of company in my life – especially when I felt like all my other relationships were slipping through my fingers. Suddenly, my students felt like the only people I could keep on side, and so I focused far too much energy on making them like me. I let smaller transgressions slide in an attempt to retain my popularity. I'd let it slide if one wasn't wearing a tie, or pretend I hadn't heard another swear. I liked being liked by them too much.

It dawned a bit too late that my students had perhaps become a bit too comfortable with me, and as the school year passed, their over-familiarity was becoming a problem. I guess while I was pretending to know what I was doing, they were acting a part at first too, trying to find their feet in the minefield of school. But September to Christmas was enough time for everyone to figure out the role they were going to sustain for the next few years – the high achiever, the mute, the class clown, the ringleader. Behaviour became a bit more difficult to manage and I was starting to struggle with the teenage inability to distinguish between the time for banter and the time to shut the fuck up and study.

I didn't really face any blatant disrespect or aggression. A couple of my students had tried to answer back, testing the boundaries, but I had learned the benefit of having naughty students on-side early on and relied on them to squash any arguments before they started. The Year 9 students who gave me my Shakespeare high were now getting a bit too relaxed, and on one occasion Lucas pulled out his phone in the middle of the lesson to send a text. I asked him to put his phone away, and he did, but I caught him two minutes later texting under the table again. When I asked him to hand his phone to me, he refused, putting the phone back into his bag, so Marvin decided to confiscate Lucas's phone for me. I continued teaching the rest of the class and turned a blind eye when he put Lucas into a headlock for challenging my decision.

The issue was that the students had started to think I was their mate rather than the teacher. And once that scale has been tipped, it is very, very hard to bring back. My Year 11 class had almost reached the end of their topic, 'Power and Conflict Poetry', and I knew revising key themes and ideas could be quite boring but time was running out, and some of the kids still thought that Wordsworth was the name of an old chain of shops that had gone into administration, so it had to be done.

'Right,' I began, 'it's really important that you know these poems inside out for your exams, so today we're going to recap some of the poems that we've studied so far.'

'Come on, Miss, that's so dry!' shouted out Naomi.

I knew the class well enough to have expected this reaction, so I just laughed and said, 'It won't be dry, sweetheart, because I've made a little game that will help you all to learn key quotes and themes!'

I pointed to the resources I had created the night before, like an overexcited Father Christmas. Apart from one or two students, no one even looked at the package on their desk.

'So . . . come on, if you open it up . . .' I urged.

A few more students reluctantly picked it up and, at snail speed, started to open it. Others, including Rafi and Edwin, still had their jackets on and were slumped back in their seats, lounging around like they were at a spa. I was hurt – after putting all that effort into the planning of the lesson, they could have at least had the decency to show some level of interest, if enthusiasm was too much to ask.

'Allow it, Miss . . .' Edwin said, cracking open a can of Coke.

They had clearly just come into the lesson in the mood to unwind, and were hoping I would tell them they could chill out for the hour. What I should have done was told Edwin to throw the drink away, picked up all the packages, stuck an essay question on the board and made them complete it in silence for the rest of the hour. But I didn't want my class to hate me. I understood that, for lots of them, school was the only time they could have the freedom to be children – how

can a bird that's born for joy sit in a cage and sing and all that
– but I also had a scheme of work to get them through, so I
pretended to be partially blind and not see the drink and
tried to persevere with my lesson plan. I pulled out a chocolate bar from my drawer and waved it around as an incentive,
but it evoked no reaction. Staring at their bored expressions,
I finally semi-snapped.

'I spent five hours making this game for you. So why
don't you sit up and stop being so ungrateful?'

My voice was more pleading than firm, but most of them
slowly, reluctantly, sat up and began to open up their enve-
lopes. I walked to my computer and pretended to type
something for a couple of minutes so I wouldn't have to
look at them, and then, when I was ready, started to circulate the classroom. They refused to engage with me, acting
like I had betrayed them. Those who continued with the
game did it as though they were doing me a favour by playing. Dejected, I waited for the hour to pass, thinking about
all the other things I could have done with my time yesterday evening.

My Year 8s came in next, excited to see me, but having
spent all my energy and enthusiasm on my Year 11s, I had
less to give them. As I took them through their starter activity, Tahir put his head on the desk and started snoring loudly
to show how tired he was. I decided to just let him sleep as
it was more peaceful that way. I always went for the easy
option because I didn't want to admit how difficult it all
was.

One afternoon found me balanced precariously on a
chair, sticking pieces of paper to a noticeboard at the back of
the classroom. They said basic things like 'don't swear' and
'don't be late' and at the top, in big letters, I wrote The Rule

Wall. I thought if there was a constant visual reminder glaring at the students, then it might infiltrate their subconscious and positively reshape their behaviour. However, when my class arrived, they didn't even notice anything had changed. They bounced around as usual in their favourite lesson of the day with their favourite teacher, while making my life a total misery in the process, and I was left staring at the Rule Wall, which now had a rogue 'L' flopping down.

On the whole, I stuck to laughing at their misdemeanours and instead put in additional hours writing their coursework for them. It was just easier. I was tired. I didn't have the energy or the guts to get into confrontations with hormonal teenagers. As the second term went on, I'd find myself looking down at my prepared scripts and realising they weren't going to cut it. However closely I'd planned my lessons, I'd probably have been better off following Ms Abbot's route and not giving an inch, or a smile, until I had control.

One spring morning, I was sitting in my classroom just before morning registration, enjoying a rare moment of solitude, when I received a phone call from my boyfriend. Like many of my twenty-two-year-old friends, it was unlike him to be awake at this ungodly hour, but I assumed he felt guilty about our recent arguments and was therefore unable to sleep. The most recent quarrel, however, had pissed me off more than usual and before I knew it, I had five fingers in the air, hysterically counting down waiting for him to Shut The Fuck Up. It's safe to say this was not well received. I picked up the phone prepared to graciously accept his apology, and was stunned when he told me that he had started seeing someone else.

I felt like I had been hit by a truck. In fact, I was completely broken. And before I even had the chance to ask any questions, the bell rang and snapped me back to life. Or away from life. Either way, I had barely hung up the phone when thirty-two of my beloved fourteen-year-olds started pouring into the classroom, racing to be first to sit next to their mates. I hadn't had the heart to insist on a seating plan yet.

I took my position at centre stage and started my performance. It was time for me to put aside my own tempestuous relationship and be the calm to their storm. In line with the frequent ironies of my life, the class was dedicated to the balcony scene of *Romeo and Juliet* and a close analysis of love. Despite the fact Romeo wanted to fuck Rosaline in the previous scene, I, with great difficulty, maintained my professionalism and tried not to taint my innocent students' analysis of the scene with my bitter and cynical perspective. I cast the roles: putting a shy and insecure but brilliant girl in the role of Juliet, next to the obvious class heart-throb as Romeo; the class clown as Mercutio and the drama queen as the Nurse. To ensure everything ran smoothly, I stood at the front of the class as the narrator and director, conducting them all. The parallels between the play and my own life would have been laughable if they weren't tragic: Juliet was not allowed out of her house, she met a man with all the lines who made constant declarations of love that he was making a few hours ago to another woman, and as expected, it all went tits up. As Romeo passionately announced that 'Love goes towards love, as schoolboys from their books, But love from love, towards school with heavy looks', I thought about how, in my case, I felt heavy from the ache of love and the books actually provided some respite from ruminating too deeply over the man who had shown little respect for what we had.

Being in the classroom was a blessing and a curse: all I wanted at that point was some privacy so I could curl up in a ball and howl, yet the excitement and smiles on my students' little faces forced me to keep going through my first real experience of heartbreak. As Romeo said goodbye to Juliet, to rapturous applause from the rest of the class, I decided it was time to bid a firm farewell to my boyfriend too.

After the break-up, I poured myself into my work more than ever before. The busier I was, the less time I spent thinking about things, the less my mind could travel to places I didn't want it to visit. The more time I spent dealing with my students' issues, the less time I had to confront any of my own. My classroom was the one place I could attempt some level of control, and the comfort of a regular structure helped me to get on with the job at hand, particularly when the rest of my life was unravelling faster than Trump's presidency. In my little bubble, the outside world didn't exist: it was sleep, work, repeat, and I liked it that way.

During the summer term, I was walking down the corridor at lunchtime in yet another skirt that was probably too short for school, plotting my next excuse to enter the Hot Maths Teacher's classroom for the third time that week, when I saw a fight break out for the first time. Two older boys were grabbing each other by the jumper and flinging each other all over the canteen. It took me a minute to establish their faces in between the punches and the kicks and I was shocked to see that my Year 9 student, Marvin, who I adored, was one of the culprits. I taught him and his younger brother, James, and although I knew Marvin was academically weak and a little naughty, he was rarely in serious trouble. As crowds began to gather, I ran closer to the scene . . . and then froze.

What was I supposed to do next?

I became hideously aware of the fact that the students involved were much taller and bigger than me, so jumping in or trying to restrain them wasn't a good idea. Luckily, two male teachers who were on lunch duty arrived at the scene a few seconds after me and pulled the boys apart, whilst one female member of staff, who I recognised as my line manager, began to shoo the crowds away. Ms Lewis was on my interview panel and her firm but gentle style was almost maternal – even for staff. She was wise and kind with a glowing smile, but also gave the impression that if you crossed her, you would regret it.

'Let's get you some lunch, Miss,' she said, as we watched the students being dragged into the isolation room. With a steady hand on my back, she guided me with ease through the large crowd and settled me into the staffroom. She put the kettle on and rummaged through the cupboard until she found a tin of biscuits. Stretching them out towards me, she said, 'They're stale . . . but they do the job.' She threw her head back with a raucous laugh that echoed around the room.

I fiddled with a cookie nervously, wondering if I was going to be told off for not handling the situation by myself. By the time she sat down in front of me, my bottom lip was quivering and I could feel the lump in my throat rising.

'I'm sorry,' I blurted. 'I wasn't really sure if I would be able to restrain them myself.'

'You wouldn't,' she said matter-of-factly, then laughed again at my expression. 'You're tiny, Miss. Even I wouldn't intervene in a fight like that. Some of our students are big and strong. We have behaviour mentors for these situations – and police officers on-site. Don't ever feel like you have to put yourself in danger. OK, darling?'

I nodded.

'You just look after yourself, Miss. The first time is always scary. Don't worry about it.'

'But you weren't scared,' I said, awestruck.

'You wouldn't know if I was. Remember, they have trust and you have cunning. You just need to find the cunning.' And with a wink, she left.

I spoke to Marvin about the incident a few days later and asked him what had happened. I had no intention of lecturing him and was genuinely concerned. He tried to laugh it off initially and told me I shouldn't worry.

'It happens, Miss,' he explained, speaking with a wisdom beyond his years. 'I'm a big man out here. Don't worry about me.'

Although his inability to comprehend the severity of the situation frustrated me, I was mildly touched by his attempt to reassure me, a grown woman, who he thought needed comfort and protection. But I persisted: I told him that I wasn't interested in what size of man he thought he was, I was asking him what compelled him to get involved in such an unnecessary conflict. Realising I wasn't going to let it go any time soon, he caved, eventually revealing this tension between them had been brewing for weeks. The other boy had an older brother who was known to be a 'gangster' around the area, which gave him the free pass to throw his weight around school. Marvin laughed to himself, disclosing that the whole thing actually started from a bad tackle at football, knowing how dramatic it sounded. Then, in a moment of rare vulnerability, he admitted that he didn't even want to fight – but also knew that walking away would be social suicide.

I sighed. Not wanting to turn the conversation too much into an interrogation and grateful for the fact he'd opened up to the extent he had, I advised him to squash it now before this escalated into something far bigger outside school.

I couldn't help making my final interjection: 'And what about James? What kind of example do you want to set for him?'

James was twelve years old and already one of my brightest students. Whip-smart, strangely wise and gentle-mannered too. You couldn't miss that they were brothers, both tall, slim and with a sort of sloping step. From behind, you could hardly tell them apart, but in a lesson, they were worlds from each other. James was conscientious and wanted to learn, whereas his brother had little interest in studying and his struggle often came out as disengagement.

And to that, Marvin stood up and retorted, 'He's a neek, Miss. Top set and that. He'll be all right.'

I observed him in fascination as he prepared to get back into character, crumpling up the report card he had been fiddling with this whole time. Shouting 'KOBE!' he shot it into the bin and as I watched him exit the room, I realised that he was playing a part too. Just like me, he was winging it. We were both probably more similar than we knew, worried that we weren't really as confident or capable as people thought we were, just faking it until we made it.

As a newly qualified teacher, acting and teaching are so inextricably linked, you can't separate the two. I was working in a profession where each day, every individual was walking around looking like they knew what they were doing and trying their best to do justice to the role they had been allocated. We were constantly performing for different audiences the whole time, be it for the kids, for our colleagues, for parents and even for inspectors.

Every situation had a real reaction that I wanted to give and then the professional reaction that I had to show. My performances were Oscar-worthy, from the little things like not revealing my fear when I saw a spider because it would escalate the students' anxiety; to the bigger issues, like when I was scared for them, lying and saying everything would be all right, even when I didn't know at the time whether that problem could be solved or not. I was always making sure that highly volatile situations remained as ordered as possible, as I was essentially, hopefully, striving to lead by example.

When you're younger, you look at adults and think they know what they're doing – and then you become an adult and realise that everyone is blagging it. We were all wearing a mask at school – even the parents wore their best clothes to hide their own fears and insecurities about being judged, or even worse, reported to social services. And when Ofsted came, students became complicit in the act, coming together with the staff to give a spectacular joint performance. As Shakespeare said, 'All the school was a stage and teachers, students and parents were merely players.' Well, he didn't quite say that, but he definitely would have had he witnessed the state of modern-day British education. We performed seven shows a day, every day, tirelessly, relentlessly . . . and there was plenty of comedy and plenty of tragedy. The emotional cost of keeping that pretence going at those times was massive.

Being a teacher was far more complicated than just teaching. That one title encompasses so many different roles. We are not allowed to have a bad day and have to continue acting way after the final chapter is read.

And with all of that burden on one individual shoulder, it was almost like we were set up to fail.

2

Failure Is Part of Life

Like any skill, my ability to teach got better with practice.

I realised I was getting quite good at the whole teacher thing during a Year 10 lesson on *An Inspector Calls*; it was all going well, until Candice unexpectedly asked me for the spelling of the word 'bourgeoisie'. Obviously, I didn't know the answer and before you question why, as an English teacher, I didn't know how to spell something, let me just say this: I didn't swallow a dictionary when I trained to be a teacher and there are some tricky words, like 'diarrhoea' and 'manoeuvre', that only psychopaths would actually know how to spell.

In my first year of teaching I'd have been horrified at being exposed so publicly, but this time I knew it was the perfect moment to embrace my inner Ms Lewis and find my cunning. 'Do you know what, darling . . . that is *such* an *excellent* question.' I passionately slammed down my board marker for additional dramatic effect and turned to face the whole class. 'I actually used to really struggle to remember the spelling of that word myself.'

I continued with such ease, I almost convinced myself that this story was true. 'It is *such* a difficult word . . . but I'm not going to tell you the answer. I want *you* to figure it out. So let's play a game: I want to see who can find "bourgeoisie" first in the dictionary.' Within seconds, the innocent souls had grabbed hold of their dictionaries and frantically started searching.

That trick worked wonders with younger students, but older years were slightly harder to please. For them, if they asked for the definition of a word that I didn't know, I would say, 'Ooh, yes . . . how do I say that in English . . . hold up, let me check with Mr Google,' which would make me seem bilingual, rather than stupid. The truth is, you could call anything a game and they would enjoy it. My personal favourite was the 'Silent Game' – everyone had to be dead silent and the first person to speak would get a fifteen-minute detention. And I swear to God, they loved it. The students trusted me blindly. As long as I could maintain the façade of being incredibly self-assured and confident in all situations, I knew I could survive.

A year in and I thought I knew it all. Ms Lewis came by my classroom to see how I was doing, and I was so excited to show her how much I had grown since the fight in the canteen.

'You keep going, Miss. A good teacher never stops learning. This is my twenty-second year here and I learn something new every day,' she said.

I had already learned so much in such a small space of time. I had built a little bubble where I thought students were learning, growing and feeling safe. The more cards and tokens of appreciation I got, the more I thought I had cracked teaching. What more was there to learn?

★　　★　　★

By the time I had weaned myself off the scripts completely, I had created a whole world within my classroom. I bought some fluffy bean bags from IKEA and utilised them in a quiet reading corner, and I kept a giant bottle of body mist by the entrance, to make sure my room still smelt like strawberries even when the boys came to lessons after football or when they were particularly gassy after lunch. I'd put up a wall of inspiring quotes, and decorated the display boards with notices and messages in fifty shades of pink. It looked like the inside of my brain, and the students loved it too because it added a splash of colour to the monotony of school. I didn't spend much time in the staffroom, but I wanted to look busy rather than anti-social, so spent any free moments I had in the day occupying myself in my classroom, planning exciting lessons for my students and cutting out a million pieces of card for their starter activities. Days would pass without thinking about the rest of the school in any detail, and while other newbies were making friends, I was becoming a solitary boat floating on a pink classroom-shaped island.

I was so focused on the students in my class, I had no energy for the teachers, and after one look in the staffroom, I knew I'd *need* energy to make friends there. A school staffroom is a little bit like one of those American high-school canteens – there are cliques, leaders, losers and stale cookies everywhere. There are the hot jocks, who are usually the PE teachers, and the Mean Girls hovering around them, usually from the Drama department, who spend their lives compensating for their loss from the National Theatre. It is characterised by inappropriate chat, lots of gossip and plenty of school politics. Walking awkwardly through the gaps between the tables to find where you would least hate to sit is enough to make you feel like you've just been picked for the Hunger Games.

I did have to go to the staffroom once a day to check my post, but it was always a brief visit, straight to my tray and then straight back out again. If I saw the Hot Maths Teacher in there, I did a little slut drop as I picked up my letters, but that was as far as my socialising skills went. I stayed out of everyone's way, minded my own business and was generally unproblematic.

That's why I was so surprised when I went down to the staffroom to collect my post one lunchtime, and the teachers on one of the tables, who had been in an animated discussion until this point, fell into a hostile silence as I walked past. It could have been my paranoia, but I could have sworn they were staring at me while I sorted through various letters and notices. As I turned to leave, I glanced over my shoulder, and my colleague, Mrs Adjei, looked at me as if she were smelling rotten fish. I had no idea what I had done, but I was too intimidated to ask, so I quickly turned around and scuttled out of the room. The next day, Mrs Adjei was giving me death stares again, and this time, I knew I wasn't making it up. I was debating whether or not to tell someone, but what could I say? 'I'd like to make a formal complaint because a teacher is giving me dirty looks'? It sounded like something a student would say – not a teacher.

But a few days later, the mystery was solved. I went down to the staffroom again and there was a suspicious looking package waiting for me in my tray. It was a large brown envelope which had a thick document inside it. Confused, I opened it, and pulled out the contents. It was a handwritten note from Mrs Adjei. 'Dear Ms Baig,' it read, 'I am writing

in regards to my son, Robbie, who is in your English class.'
Robbie, Robbie, Robbie . . . the name rang a bell. I wracked
my brain trying to think of who it was, and then identified
him as a quiet boy in my new Year 7 class. He was polite and
unassuming – he seemed to be enjoying the lessons but was
the type of student who would get quite anxious if you
picked him to answer a question or read aloud. The letter
outlined all the reasons why Mrs Adjei was convinced that
Robbie wasn't being supported in my class and contained
photocopied pages of his book, highlighted and annotated,
indicating where she felt like he could have done better –
she had even circled words that he had misspelled that I
hadn't corrected. I didn't want to read all of it in public, so I
quickly stuffed it back into the envelope and turned to leave.
In the doorway, I bumped into Mrs Adjei, looking intense,
and mumbling an agitated 'Excuse me', I returned to my
classroom and sank in my chair, tossing the letter onto my
desk.

After I had recovered from the initial shock of it, I read
through her complaints in detail, and then composed an
email, addressing her concerns. I explained that we had a
policy in English to not correct every single spelling as it
could often be demotivating for students, so instead we
focused on words that had rules and patterns. She didn't
reply – well, at least not electronically – but the next day,
another, fresh, handwritten note was lurking in my tray. I
stopped replying and hoped they would go away, but I
started to receive the notes more frequently, at least three
times a week, telling me a line-by-line analysis of what
Robbie struggled with in my lessons that day and how
anxious he was feeling. As she got more comfortable, the
letters became more aggressive, and could be comparable

only to death threats or ransom notes. It added to my anxiety quite considerably and shunned me even further away from the staffroom.

Clearly my hunch about being a misfit in the teacher world was spot on, so instead, when I needed a change of scenery, I went down to visit the canteen staff and caretakers, who were always happy to see me and seemed to have more fun than any other department in the school. Our canteen was incredible and embodied everything I had loved about the school on my interview day. I was working in a school that celebrated – and more importantly embraced – the cultural diversity of the students as part of the tapestry of the school, and it was woven in seamlessly. We all looked forward to having well-seasoned chicken and rice and peas with all the trimmings on a Wednesday lunchtime, and samosas and hot wings at break that were flavoured to the palate of the children who came from homes where food was spicy. Jackie, the head of the canteen team, was a Jamaican woman who had basically adopted me from the minute she saw me. Every time she saw me approaching the dining hall, she looked me up and down, appalled, and shouted, 'You need to look after yourself and fatten yourself up, girl!' before thrusting a free carton of chocolate milk into my hands.

I was particularly close with a young guy called Ali, who had moved over to Britain from Somalia a few years prior to me joining the school and worked in the kitchen. On the weekend, he rode a bicycle for Deliveroo, which he assured me saved him a fortune on a gym membership, and at the end of each month, he sent his wages to his parents back home.

Ali was the best person to disclose my innermost fears to, not just because I knew he wouldn't judge me, but because he had a natural way of calming me down and found my constant panic attacks hilarious.

Every day without fail, he would say, 'Looking lovely, Friend. And how are you feeling?'

I would reply, 'Stressed, Ali,' to which he would respond, with an Ali-special positive spin: 'Don't stress, do your best.'

I spent so many hours in that one building, it was just nice to feel like somebody cared about me, and even a simple question asking me how I was made all the difference. Over time, I grew to notice when students looked like they needed the same care and attention – the ones who started coming a couple of minutes before the bell or those who deliberately took an eternity to pack their bags at the end of the lesson. They only wanted a minute of respite like I got from Ali and the rest of the non-teaching staff, and the trusted counsel I got from Ms Lewis.

I got used to tidying up after a lesson, or preparing for my next class, whilst simultaneously listening to the students' chatter, as they started basing themselves more and more in my classroom. At break-times and lunchtimes, I would let someone trustworthy sit by my computer to be the DJ and play the latest 'bangers', pretending to be outraged at the lyrics even though I had been listening to them myself on my way into school.

I sat with them, laughed with them, offered them life advice and, at one point, I even started running a free under-ground tuition service, where I helped students complete their homework from other subjects. We had fallen in step with each other. And I could hear through the paper-thin walls that my colleagues were creating the same buzz in their rooms too. We each crafted a sanctuary within our four walls where we could try and offer support to the students who came through the doors.

I guess that's what great teachers do. They have a magical ability to conjure joy into their students' lives, regardless of how they feel themselves, or what else is going on in their world. When I came into school at 7 a.m., Ms Lewis would already be in her office, waving to me as I walked past, and by the time I was leaving, she was still there. Our students didn't want to go home either. At the end of each day, many of them used to stay until 7 p.m. doing their homework, reading, chatting, and sometimes we would order boxes of pizzas, knowing that for some of these students, it was their only meal. We always hear stories of students who don't want to go to school, and pretend to have tummy-aches to get out of submitting homework, but in our case, school was their safe haven. It took me a long time to really understand that the care I tried to show the kids sometimes wasn't replicated anywhere else in their lives, and for many, school was the only place where they found guidance, discipline and fun.

My most important advice for new teachers would be to find time for the one-to-one chats, as they allow you to get to know the students on a personal level. You learn a lot about your school by listening to the students; they can be innocent and insightful in equal measure. A fourteen-year-old can be more self-aware and perceptive than any adult, and even the quietest student can tell you more about your school – and sometimes even about you – than you would ever expect.

News spreads quickly in schools, and the news of my classroom being the new hangout didn't take long to circulate.

Students who I didn't even teach would turn up at lunchtime to come and join the fun, and sometimes would find excuses to leave their own classes during lesson time to see what we were getting up to. I planned interactive activities which meant my room was usually vibrant and noisy, and students from other classes would be drawn in by the sound of chaos. I let them join, mostly because my own students performed visibly better in front of 'guests' so the interruption actually benefited me. Some students from neighbouring classrooms would take extra-long toilet breaks just for a couple of minutes of entertainment, whilst others would pretend to have a music lesson. One boy, Abdullah, loved our class so much, he went the extra mile to ensure he got kicked out of his lesson by whatever means possible so that he could come and sit in ours. At first, I felt sorry for him because it seemed that his teacher would need very little excuse to evict him, but it happened so frequently that it became fairly obvious those removals were premeditated. I let him stay, though I probably shouldn't have, because in my head, as long as he was learning, I didn't mind which classroom he did it in, and he was soon an honorary member of my class.

One lunchtime, he sat with us, entertaining everyone as he always did, talking about some older girls he had tried to chat up on the high road. The conversation quickly moved up a gear when he started suggesting which teacher he would set me up with in school, and before I could stop him, he began reeling off names of male staff, loudly eliminating those who were too old, too moody, or those who wore strange shoes. The other students were in hysterics at my aghast expressions, the girls particularly outraged on my behalf.

As if he had had an epiphany, Abdullah blurted out, 'Mr Clarke!' Then, after a moment of evaluating this hypothetical union, he added, '. . . but he's married. Though he has taken off his ring recently. And he's been angrier than usual. Bare shouting and that. I think you got a chance, Miss.'

'How do you know I'm not married, Abdullah?' I challenged.

He casually responded, 'Nah, you're not married, Miss. You're way too happy. Dem people miserable.' He paused for a second, contemplating thoughtfully. 'How about Mr Wilson? He's cool.' I tried to look as nonchalant as possible. The Hot Maths Teacher. What did they know about him?

Suddenly, from the corner of the room, a soft voice emerged. Ceylan, who had hardly ever uttered three syllables, said, 'Miss wouldn't marry Mr Wilson. He always says "I done". Miss hates it when people say that.'

I couldn't help smiling. Like wet clay, students absorbed every word we said, even those intended as throwaway comments. We could mould their minds to believe in themselves, or crush their spirit with a single harsh word. Particularly for the students who came from households that didn't sit together around a dinner table discussing the news or current affairs, our daily interactions and conversations were where they learned about the world and shaped their ideologies and moral compass. But with that knowledge came the importance of using our power wisely. If we could make or break a child, we needed to be very careful of what we said and how we said it.

'Anyways, I swear Mr Clarke's banging that art teacher?' Abdullah volunteered instead.

With a laugh, I told the mini tabloids to pack away and start making their way to their next lesson.

James was waiting by the door, ready with a carton of juice in one hand, a pen in the other. You shouldn't have favourites as teachers, but I did have a soft spot for him. I was aware he wasn't perfect in all of his other lessons – as his report card showed – but in English, he was incredibly bright, and eager to learn the persuasive devices that would one day help him to become Prime Minister. While his brother was getting into fights and sauntering between lessons, James was set on a different path. He was sporty enough to be considered 'cool' by his peers, but would happily lie on the bean bag in the corner of my room and read for hours. I gave him my own copy of *The Catcher in the Rye* to take home and he practically gobbled it up, and came back two days later eager to discuss what he thought was wrong with Holden Caulfield. He had all the promise in the world, lacking nothing except a bit of guidance and support.

His Head of Year was Mr Abara, a middle-aged man who looked a bit like a general and acted like it too. He gave out detentions like they were lollipops and never wavered from routine and rules. I understood why – teaching was hard enough, managing an entire year was nearly impossible. Head of Year was a position we were all meant to aspire to, but it came with a ridiculous list of demands, from managing all the teachers to keeping on top of mountains of admin, to overseeing discipline and development. It took absolute organisation and focus, so it wasn't all that surprising most of them acted like they'd been through training with the Commandos. It also wasn't surprising that they rarely had time to give one student a lot of attention. With Mr Abara missing in action, I had decided to give some special attention to James. He would be my success story.

At the start of my second year of teaching, and James's second year in the school, we established a routine. Twice a week, he'd drop by at the end of school and we'd spend an hour looking at his homework and chatting – about school, about his aspirations, and about his family. He was incredibly close to his mum, and still called her 'Mummy' which always seemed funny coming from a six-foot-tall boy, but she had her own issues, stemming from a series of relationships that constantly broke down, taking time away from her children. She would rather have the children out of the house so she could get some private time with a man, but the street wasn't exactly a safe place for the boys to be. James wanted to learn, wanted to do well, but sometimes his friends and, to be honest, his family, tempted him in another direction.

Keeping a close eye on James also served a double purpose, as he was my secret spy, monitoring what his older brother, Marvin, was getting up to. James worried about him and spoke at great length about Marvin's latest antics. The most recent case was Marvin getting arrested in JD Sports as he tried to shoplift some new trainers – mum was at work, dad wasn't around, so the Assistant Head, Mr Fieldhouse, had to collect him at 9 p.m. from the police station. I promised James I would speak to his brother and try to knock some sense into him, without disclosing that James had confided in me, of course. Looking back, I guess this was the first time I really felt a maternal instinct kick in – a desire to alleviate his worries and protect him.

On a late afternoon of a particularly draining day, maybe a week or so after the incident, I was packing away my belongings and changing into my trainers for the commute home when James came into my classroom. He asked if he could revise for a bit in my room and, recognising something was wrong, I sat back down on the student chair beside him, temporarily pushing the fantasies of Mum's hot dinner to the side of my mind. Sitting next to the children made a big difference. It broke down the invisible barrier between teachers and students, removed the power imbalance, and allowed students to open up freely.

I pulled out a random book to mark, and tried to sound casual.

'So, what are you revising for?' I continued flicking and ticking through the pages. 'Anything I can help with?'

'I got a History test, Miss.' He continued reading the textbook, his face in a deep frown.

'But that's a Geography textbook, sweetheart.' I put my pen down and turned to face him directly, and he looked at the front of his textbook in a panic. I started to laugh, and he did too.

'Go on, spill. What's going on?' He shifted uncomfortably in his chair.

'It's not important, Miss,' he tried to look nonchalant.

'Well . . . you're hiding in my room after school on a Friday afternoon, so it's got to be something,' I replied.

'I just . . . can't go home yet,' he said quietly. 'Marvin got into some beef . . . like, an argument . . . with some boys from Wood Green yesterday.' He stopped suddenly.

'Did you think I didn't know what "beef" meant?' I looked at him deadpan, and he laughed again, relaxing.

'Nah, Miss. I know you're from the ends.'

'This is true. So anyway . . . Marvin got into . . . some beef . . .'

'And obviously, I had to back him. But now . . . you know, I can't go home at normal time in case they're like . . . waiting for me. So I just want to wait for a bit. If that's OK?'

He fiddled with the corners of the pages in the textbook until he was holding the small fragments in his fingers. I tried to maintain an expression of calmness as best as I could, even though I was horrified. What we were actually talking about was serious – yet James didn't seem scared, just a bit tense. Whether this happened all the time or not, he'd found and followed what he thought was the necessary protocol to ensure he got back home safely by leaving at an unpredictable time each day. He spoke with the sort of indifference that would be unthinkable to someone not from his world.

I wondered if things had always been like this and I had just been shielded from it – perhaps because I had the privilege of my parents picking me up and dropping me off at school and not letting me out of the house any other time. I hated them for it back then – thinking they were so unfair – but I understood and appreciated the value of it now. James was a child. He shouldn't have had anything to worry about except rolling around in mud and jumping in puddles, but his experience had hardened him. Although he insisted if he left at 6 p.m. he would be OK, I reported the situation to Mr Abara, who immediately organised for a cab to take him home safely.

As I watched him walk towards the cab, head down, it felt a bit like we were giving him an umbrella to use in a storm: an illusion of shelter and perhaps some level of protection, but it wouldn't take much for it to disintegrate, leaving a vulnerable little boy at the threat of drowning.

A few days later, we were all involved in preparing for an event I loathed when I was a student: Sports Day. I wasn't particularly sporty, it would mess up my hair and it generally seemed like a total waste of time. I have many talents, but balancing an egg on a spoon and running at the same time is not one of them. As a teacher, however, I loved it. We had no lessons until lunchtime, the kids were really excited and I got to spend a few hours perving over the Hot Maths Teacher. Whilst most teachers assumed the position of crowd control, I usually usurped the role of the cheerleader, chanting for my students from the side.

Towards the end of the event, there were always a series of teacher games. It wasn't obligatory for teachers to participate, but many did, because the kids looked forward to watching and mocking the staff. English teachers had usually sneaked off by this point, but it was my favourite part of the whole day.

That summer, I was positioned on the front row of the audience, watching the line-up of a teacher relay race intently. James, who was in the row behind me, shouted, 'Aren't you going to run, Miss?' and I turned around and smiled, thinking I wouldn't even run to catch the bus and said, 'No, sweetie, these heels aren't made for running.' As all the participating teachers stood in teams, with their leaders standing shoulder to shoulder, Mr Clarke got on the microphone as the commentator, providing a thorough analysis of each participant. 'Firstly, Mr Brooks – with the advantage of being a PE teacher. And next, we can see Mr Fieldhouse getting into line looking like he is ready to WIN,' his voice boomed around the astroturf. 'Look at that. What a sport. But can he beat Mr Abara?' The crowds went wild at the sight of the Assistant Head and Head of Year 8 loosening their ties and stepping into position. 'Who's that? Could this be true? That's right, kids, it's Ms Williams. Ready to put these men in their place!' Ms Williams, from the classroom opposite mine, waved at the students as she jogged on the

spot, warming up her body before her run. Hot Maths
Teacher was helping them all get organised, handing the
teachers their batons.

'Oh! Is that Mr Wilson getting involved in the relay?
Yes . . . yes . . . no! He's just being the good Samaritan that
he always is.' Hot Maths Teacher looked towards the tent in
which Mr Clarke was clearly having a ball and chuckled,
then continued to get on with the job at hand. As the kids
started chanting for him to get involved, Mr Clarke got back
onto the microphone, 'Don't worry, guys, Mr Wilson just
wants to make sure the rest of the teachers have a chance!
No offence, Mr Abara.' The students roared with laughter
and so did the staff. As the sound of the gun shot went off
and the teachers started running, the crowd erupted in a
chorus of chants.

'Come on, Ms Williams!' I shouted, obviously supporting
my own department. The race was over pretty quickly and,
as expected, Mr Brook's team emerged victorious. The
students whooped in delight, as everyone got ready for the
next game.

'Right, everyone!' Mr Clarke declared. 'The next game
is the penalty shootout. Each teacher has three shots to get
the football into the goal. We have Yasser, our star sports-
man, as our goalkeeper. Give them a wave, son.' Yasser
waved to applause. 'The teacher who scores the most goals
wins. So . . . who is going to take part?' The usual suspects
began to line up again. 'OK . . . quiet please! Let's see . . .
so we have a strong line-up here. The competition will be
fierce. Mr Lever has decided to give it another go to try and
redeem himself.' Mr Lever played to his crowds by flexing
his muscles. 'And . . . Mr Wilson is also going to take part!
Go on, Sir!' I was busy watching the Hot Maths Teacher

take his position when I heard, 'Miss Baig. Why don't you get up here and show us what you've got?'

Startled, I looked towards Mr Clarke grinning ear to ear, then I turned to look at the students whose eyes were on me. A penalty shootout? Were they having a fucking laugh? I didn't want to look like a spoilsport, so there was no other option. I stepped forward onto the pitch.

The crowds went wild. It was a great feeling. This is what Ronaldo must feel like, I thought. How hard could kicking a ball into a net be anyway?

The football was placed on the ground in front of me and adrenaline was surging through my body. This could be massive for my cool ratings. Trying to look graceful yet athletic, I took one step back, and then swung my foot as hard as possible. The impact on the ball seemed minimal – it moved a pathetic few yards forward and there was a disappointed groan from the audience. The impact on my toe, however, was huge. My toenail was broken. A stabbing pain shot through my foot and up my leg, and I was immediately worried my pedicure would never look the same again. The crowd didn't seem to care about my injury because they were already chanting, 'AGAIN! AGAIN!' This was ruthless.

I hobbled back to my original position, smiling through my pain, when a voice asked, 'Are you OK, Miss?' I turned and saw Hot Maths Teacher next to me, looking concerned.

'I'm fine!' I replied in a high-pitched voice. God, he was fit. All the pain seemed to have disappeared in an instant. He looked relieved.

'Good.' He smiled, and gave me space for my next shot. I had a renewed motivation. Taking a deep breath, I composed myself and looked down at the ball. Then at the goal. Then back down at the ball, calculating the exact angle and strength I would need to bypass the goalkeeper. 3 . . . 2 . . . 1. I stepped back and lunged forward. With my new energy, the heel of my shoe sank into the grass, and all that emerged was my bare foot. My exposed toes collided with the ball, which moved towards the goal and I was convinced that my entire foot was broken. The students were in hysterics and so was Mr Clarke, his laughter echoing through the speakers.

When you first start teaching, the world of the classroom is so all-consuming you don't give that much thought to the rest of the school. You know who the Head is, and that your line-manager is someone you shouldn't piss off. You've worked out quite early on what teachers to avoid (the spitty French teacher) and who to keep on side (the photocopying lady). But you're so focused on getting through each lesson, you don't think about the fact those children leave your class and go into someone else's. That student you have a soft spot for is a nightmare in History, and the one you struggle with is shining elsewhere.

A few months after my conversation with James, I tottered down to our weekly staff briefing, took my seat on the 'English' row and was inconspicuously scanning the room for the Hot Maths Teacher, when the Head announced that one of our students was going to be excluded. My attention returned to the front of the hall where he was standing, and I felt alert for the first time ever in one of these meetings. This was usually my designated time to have open-eyed naps. The Head fiddled through some papers, whispered something to Mr Fieldhouse next to him, and then looked back up to our expectant faces: 'The student is in Year 8.' He looked at his notes once again. 'James Amin.'

I was sure I had misheard. His words seemed to blur into nothingness as he continued to describe how James had brought fireworks into the school with a box of matches and it was a welfare issue that could not be overlooked. I was in a state of shock. The same James who volunteered to help me hand the books out when I wasn't well, and beamed when I gave him the smiley face on his test results, was 'a danger to other students'. I couldn't believe that the school was even considering taking away the one safety network and security blanket from his life.

Although until now I had deliberately kept a low profile, particularly from the senior leadership team, I knew I had to do everything in my power to keep James in school. I went straight to Mr Abara's office, pushing open the door and striding in like Superman.

Mr Abara looked up and placed his pen carefully down, beckoning to the chair opposite him.

'Sit down, please, Miss.'

'Please don't exclude James,' I launched into my defence. I begged him to reconsider, arguing that he was just a young child who had simply made a big mistake, that he was doing very well academically. I said he was gifted in English, and that I thought he could go to university. I put everything out there, and was almost on my knees.

He heard me but didn't quite listen, clearly waiting to return to his own pressing workload, and explained that James had put other students and himself at risk and we could not give other students the impression that this behaviour would be tolerated; it would set the wrong precedent.

Mr Abara apologised and I remember replying with, 'It's OK' – but I lied. Nothing was OK. I felt utterly powerless in the school hierarchy. My lack of experience and young age meant that my voice wasn't heard. I was seen as well-meaning but naïve.

I couldn't sleep for days, replaying the incident over and over again in my mind, agonising over what I could have done differently. I kicked myself for not having stronger arguments, statistics, copies of his work or something to highlight that this decision was not in his best interest. As an English teacher, I should have used Aristotle's persuasive triad, a mixture of an appeal to emotion (pathos), reason (logos) and morality (ethos). I had only used pathos. I felt pathetic. Most of all, I felt like I had failed to help James.

For once, I couldn't face my students, and didn't have the answers to the barrage of questions I feared they would ask about James's exclusion. It was too difficult and I just needed a pause . . . a bit of a breather. I decided it would be best to go to the staffroom and try to form connections with the staff. I needed adult company – and to speak to somebody who would empathise. My friends would try to listen and would care, but they didn't know James or the school. They wouldn't understand. I was lonely, and it was my fault, so thought it was time I tried to make some friends at work.

I've made many bad decisions in life, but the decision to socialise was definitely up there. The speculation around James's exclusion only served to heighten my own emotions. I sat with a group of teachers, including Mr Clarke and Ms Bloome from my department, and tried my best to remain neutral in the discussion.

'I was on a training course all week,' Mr Clarke said, between mouthfuls of falafel, 'so I only found out this morning. What did he actually do?'

'Not sure, but I'll miss him,' Ms Bloome said, and I made a slight sound of agreement. 'What surprises me is that his brother is still here.'

I resumed my silence. Mr Lever came to join the table, and we shuffled over to make room for him.

'What are we talking about, guys?' he asked, putting on the deep, growly voice he always did when women were around.

'The boy who was excluded,' Mr Clarke replied. 'James. Did you teach him?'

'Yeah, nasty little thing,' he said. 'Didn't you hear what he did? Brought explosives to school.'

'It was a firework. It was hardly an AK-47, or a bomb, or something!' I snapped. The words came out harsher than I had intended. He didn't reply and there was the type of awkward silence that makes you wish that the earth would swallow you up. I waited until it didn't seem like I was sulking and then politely walked out of the staffroom, vowing to never return.

I spent the rest of the day shifting between rage and sadness. My distress must have been quite visible because Mr Thorne, the Head, wrote me an email afterwards, checking to see if I was OK and reassuring me that it was natural to feel this way.

Mr Thorne was highly intelligent, experienced and intuitive and I had the utmost respect for him. Our school had been failing when I was growing up. When my sister went there, it only had a 17 per cent pass rate at GCSE, but then Mr Thorne swept in and completely turned it around, even going on to win a CBE for his exceptional contribution to education. I tried to tell myself that if he had made this decision, he must have known something which I simply couldn't see.

I know my anger was probably misdirected at Mr Lever, and it is unfair to blame what happened on any individual. It wasn't really the school's fault either. My decade in teaching correlated with the decade of austerity, and budget cuts, which at that point were only at the initial stages of being implemented but would later go on to uproot education at an exponential rate. Financial restraints meant there were fewer staff, teaching more lessons, with bigger class sizes, and decreased resources. Any spare moments were spent trying to unearth some pennies to purchase more stationery so every student had at least a pencil to write with and there were barely enough dictionaries for one between two. We often spent hours rummaging through old cupboards, looking for copies of books that didn't have entire chapters missing, so the students could at least access their syllabus. All schools were heavily underfunded, and the fact that there was not enough money for basic necessities meant there was certainly nothing left for luxuries, such as the provision to support student behaviour and mental health: mentors, pastoral staff, on-site counsellors and a strong pastoral curriculum.

If we had the funding for early intervention, we would be able to implement effective monitoring to stop the students from dipping, and spot signs of disengagement earlier. But we simply did not have the money, space, time, resources or energy to do that. The onus to help the students fell solely on us in a structure that was already stretched thin. Each time the Education Secretary changed, the list of our duties grew. Teachers were held responsible if anything tragic occurred and the catastrophic impact of austerity was brushed under the carpet.

James was definitely not our first or last exclusion, but he was the first who I considered my own. And because he was so high-achieving and talented, his tragic downfall felt greater. He came back to visit a couple of times, though he probably wasn't allowed, and then, after a couple of months, he stopped coming back altogether.

If James existed in a world where schools had enough money, he might not have slipped through the net. We might have been able to put in preventative strategies to catch him. But when that net was so widely spread, and one teacher was forced to adopt so many roles, it was an impossible thing to do.

James wasn't even an obvious risk. He had a badly behaved brother, missed a few grades in some classes and perhaps hung out with a few people he shouldn't. But if someone as bright as him could still get pulled enough in the wrong direction, then we were in real trouble.

I knew it would be unfair to expect the school to simply pour all their limited resources into protecting one James, because if all the energy went into the Jameses, then who would look after the Ceylans? Instead, we were trained to forgo one James for the greater good and we learned the hard way that failure is just a part of life, and always a part of teaching. I knew I had to learn to detach and not take every failure or mistake to heart, or else it would be impossible to move on. With that thought in my mind, I forced myself to adopt a more positive outlook, and do my best for my other students. As Paulo Coelho said, 'My heart might be bruised, but will recover and become capable of seeing beauty of teaching once more.' Well, he didn't say teaching – but you know what I mean. Anyway, I decided to face the future, rather than wallow in the past. All we could do was make the best we could with what we had and, in some sense, relinquish control.

★ ★ ★

My classroom looked different after James's expulsion. It didn't emit that feeling of being a refuge from the outside world and had lost the sparkle and glitter I had tried so desperately to bring into the children's lives. I knew I had to bring it back.

I perched on the edge of my desk, watching my students copy down learning objectives in silence. I looked around at them, re-evaluating the setting. The Rule Wall stared back at me; the soulless rigidity of the words stood out even more now, little things compared to the unpredictable reality of our experience. Suddenly, 'don't eat, don't be late' seemed futile. I asked the students to put their pens down. With slight confusion, they looked up at me, wondering what they had done wrong. I walked over to the display board and tore it down – ripping off the rules one by one.

'This is your classroom,' I told them, 'and I need you to feel comfortable here. There is no point in me telling you the rules. You know not to be late to the lesson, you know not to swear. What I need is for you to tell me what the one most important thing is that will make you feel safe, confident and ready to learn. I want you to come up to the board and write down that one rule, then pass the pen to someone else.'

They were silent and unsure about what was happening. I was being vulnerable . . . but this was important. I turned around and started them off: 'Don't stress, do your best.' Handing two markers to the children closest to me, I walked away to let them get on with it.

It was clear to me that however good we were as teachers, whatever our classrooms were like, we would come up against problems that we wouldn't be able to do anything about. The realisation that we were fallible disheartened me for a while, but I had to learn to let go of the things that had gone wrong and focus on the things that I could control. Sometimes things don't work out – that's just life – but I was still going to give it my bloody best shot. The failure to protect James meant that I would do everything in my power to protect the others with every fibre of my being.

It was inevitable that such fire and ferocity in my belly would eventually end up taking its toll on me.

3

Look After Yourself

I was impressed by how quickly I had got to the point in my career where I spent every day fantasising about making it to the final bell, to Friday, to the end of term. I was twenty-three years old and wishing my life away and, with each day, getting closer to death.

Don't get me wrong, I wasn't bored. My first couple of years at the school passed by in a frantic rush. I was rushing to plan my lessons, rushing to write reports, rushing to meetings and briefings, rushing to my break and lunch duties . . . and generally just rushing. And then there was marking. Imagine thirty-two children, writing three pages of mostly incomprehensible work, five times a day – not the type of work that can be ticked and crossed, might I add – and you're expected to transform it into lyrical prose. Quite a challenge, wouldn't you agree? And even if I did hypothetically manage to conquer all 480 pages (a feat I never accomplished) another 480 pages of drivel would be ready and waiting to be marked by the end of the day. It was like climbing a ladder, but when you got to the top, it grew taller. In fact, it didn't just grow taller, it suddenly released a snake, which wrapped itself around your neck, sucked the remaining air out of you, and then watched your lifeless limbs slide down all the way to the bottom again. So, a sadistic version of Snakes and Ladders is the best I can do to describe marking – but without the kinky pleasure.

And before anyone tries to label me lazy, let's do the Maths together, shall we? Let's pretend for the sake of this argument that one book takes 10 minutes to mark (it doesn't, it takes more like 20). If we multiply that by 160 books, that is 1,600 minutes, which is just under 27 hours of marking per day.

Now, I know some people may think I'm exaggerating. So, let's pretend each book takes 5 minutes to flick and tick. If we multiply 5 minutes by 160 books, that's 800 minutes of marking per day, which is just over 13 hours per day.

Fine. Let's now take the ABSOLUTE MINIMUM and say that each child only produces 1 page of work, and each page takes only 2 minutes to mark, and only 25 students are present that day. Even in this case, 2 minutes x 25 pages x 5 lessons per day is still 250 minutes. That's *still* over 4 hours per day of marking.

And that's not including homework, set once a week. And that's not even including assessments, which were set once every half-term to be completed on separate sheets of paper, that I had to mark in detail, and upload the results to the department's tracking Excel spreadsheet.

And all of this means one thing: overtime.

Teachers are not paid for any overtime, so it is an unwritten and unspoken form of overtime only found in the teaching profession. Before we even consider the planning and admin and photocopying and one-to-ones with parents and children, let's just focus on the marking for now and just let the sheer absurdity and unreasonableness sink in. So, the next time you are about to open your mouth and tell teachers about their holidays, take a minute, pause, reflect, then . . . don't.

Regardless, I was plagued by a sudden pang of guilt at the image of the lonely books left in my cupboard in solitary confinement. I carried the boxes of exercise books home with the most noble intentions, but ended up staring at them guiltily day after day, unable to bring myself to touch them but equally unable to enjoy myself when I knew they had to be marked. I carried the same boxes back to school after the holiday in the same state that they had left in.

At home I procrastinated, but staying after school to do marking offered no greater inspiration. Or, at least, not the type I was looking for. On one occasion, I went searching for an empty classroom where no one would disturb me. Imagine my horror, then, when I opened a door to find two teachers passionately snogging – the female had her skirt hitched up and seemed surprisingly unperturbed that her arse was on display. I didn't pause to see the extent of their indiscretion and, mortified, I quickly shut the door and tried to block out the scene from my mind. I never told a single soul. You don't grass on your horny colleagues in teaching (as long as both parties are consenting adults). Unless you're writing a book, of course.

In a desperate attempt to reduce my marking pile, I volunteered to teach bottom set – the advantage being that there were fewer students, who were less motivated, so produced less work. However, this strategic plan brought unforeseen consequences, such as when young Daniel asked me, 'If my grandma is dead, am I still alive?' For a minute, I questioned whether there was some hidden genius behind this thought, but alas, no. Further enquiry revealed that both of his grand-mothers were, in fact, alive. After a few months, I missed the stimulation of my old set and moved back, marking be damned.

As a last resort, I asked Mike, the school caretaker, for a key to the storage cupboard in my room so I could keep my unmarked exercise books firmly locked away, only bringing them out for lessons. Most kids didn't really care about their books and only wanted assessments marked anyway; you could mark with the most intricate detail but they would skim past all of it just to get to the grade at the bottom. At least the books were safe from prying managers who like to nose around to see if we are doing our job properly. I let them stack up for days and then weeks, praying that no one ever found them.

In case you're wondering, this isn't the decision-making process of someone who's coping. In that cupboard, along with the books, I had firmly locked away my anxieties, inse-curities and fears, and if anyone ever opened it, I would be confronted by the chaos that had become my life. But as long as no one entered Bluebeard's basement, my secret was safe and my reputation intact.

As a matter of fact, while unmarked homework stacked up and my mental health spiralled, my reputation was blossom-ing. My PowerPoints had been shared on the staff drive by Ms Lewis for other teachers to use, my first lesson observa-tion was 'very impressive' and I had even been invited to deliver a session for the English department on how we could use technology to enhance our teaching.

The idea came about when I was 'coincidentally' passing by the Hot Maths Teacher's classroom and saw him using a

very clever piece of machinery. It was the perfect opportunity for me to pick his brains, all in the name of 'professional development' of course. He introduced me to the
'visualiser', a device that allows you to project a student's
work onto the whiteboard, and I went straight to my Head
of Department, Ms Kowalski, to share my new discovery. Ms
Kowalski looked a bit like Elsa from *Frozen,* except in a suit,
and though she didn't have the warmth of Ms Lewis, she was
one of the few people that could keep such a large faculty in
check (and trust me, I saw a few try). She was always keen to
hear new ideas and suggested that I do a presentation on how
the visualiser could best be utilised for our subject.

It all felt very exciting. This was my chance to impress
everyone and show them what I was really made of. My dad
always quotes his own invented proverb, which roughly
translates to 'Don't use a leaf to wipe your arse when it is just
a short walk to the lake', and though this may mean nothing
to you, it is actually quite profound. In actual fact, it means
that if you plan to do something, do it properly.

In this spirit, I began extensive preparation for my five-
minute presentation. I created colourful booklets and printed
enough copies for everyone. The accompanying PowerPoint
outlined instructions and example activities of how it could
be incorporated within literacy starter activities. I rehearsed
my script on my students, my family, and to myself in a
mirror. I had got it into my head that this was my only
opportunity to blow everyone away with how creative,
organised, smart and efficient I was.

But when the moment arrived, the hall was not buzzing,
as I had envisaged. At 4.30 p.m. exactly, Ms Kowalski began
with the opening speech, updating the faculty – which
consisted of twenty-five women – on the plans for the

following weeks and reminding them of important dead-lines. I sat, with butterflies and diarrhoea in my belly, eagerly waiting for the announcement of my name and the impending awe and respect of my peers. I was ready.

Of course, in every school, there is always that one teacher who deliberately asks a question just to be difficult, and delay everyone from going home for as long as possible. In mine, it was Ms D'Alessio, and right on cue, she put her hand up seeking clarification about something blindingly obvious. This led to the usual collective metaphoric death of souls around the room and all the women sat, bored and resentful, waiting for it to be over. Usually, I would be one of them, but today was my debutante arrival. I was shuffling around in my seat, with a pounding heart, waiting for Ms Kowalski to finish so I could stand up on the podium and do my presentation, all eyes on me. I was the lead character in all my school plays, Head Girl at school, and I was ready for my stardom here too. I knew I could do this.

Finally, the moment arrived. I got up and walked to the front of the room, my legs slightly trembling beneath me. I passed the booklets to Ms Kowalski, who smiled encouragingly and started handing them out. I looked up, ready to start. I cleared my throat and started speaking.

'Good afternoon, everyone. I am so excited to be doing this presentation . . .' I scanned the room. Everyone looked disinterested, bordering on disgusted. Some were even looking at the clock.

I continued, 'As Couros once said, technology will not replace great teachers but in the hands of great teachers can be transformational.' I looked up again. Worse. Now, one teacher was hiding her phone in her lap, texting, and another doing a fairly shitty job of stifling a yawn.

'Umm . . . I . . .' God, what was after the quote? My mind had gone completely blank and I could not remember for the life of me what came next. I caught Ms Lewis's eye in the audience, and she looked concerned. My body was having some sort of visceral reaction. The paper I was holding was shaking and I could have sworn the microphone was picking up the thumping sound of my heart. 'I wanted to talk to you all about the vishaza . . .' As I sped through the key word of the whole presentation, it sounded more like 'vajazzle' than 'visualiser'. And that was it: I was completely thrown. I forgot what came next, and as I searched for the words on the page, my voice began to shake. I strongly considered admitting defeat and shuffling back to my seat. My very visible breakdown did at least prompt my colleagues to sit up just a little bit more, with a mixture of guilt and concern. I do know that they didn't mean to be so unsupportive. It wasn't personal to me – the cynicism towards any additional demands made on their time was engrained in their spirits. But it was too late; I was already past the point of no return. I couldn't do it. Any of it.

I somehow mumbled my way to the end of the presentation, and the faculty clapped in pity. Ms Kowalski returned to the podium and thanked me for my effort and time, giving my shoulder a little squeeze, and I collected my discarded booklets from the tables while everyone filtered out of the room, so that I didn't have to meet anyone's eye. I had fucked up many times in front of the kids who did not know any better, but this time, I had exposed myself and stood naked and vulnerable in front of adults who had seen right through me – and I felt absolutely crushed.

★   ★   ★

Back in my classroom, I screwed up the booklets and chucked them, one by one, into the bin. I would have burned them if I could. I wouldn't mind messing something up that I wasn't prepared for, but in this instance, I had gone above and beyond – and that made this humiliation all the more difficult to digest. I took off my cardigan, which was now covered in sweat patches, and, feeling repulsed by myself, kicked off my heels. There I was, reaching under my desk on all fours, rummaging through my secret stash of shoes for my trainers, when I heard a cough at the door. I bounced up, banging my head on the desk as I did so, and saw Aurea, the English teacher from the classroom opposite me, standing in my doorway.

Aurea was only a few years older than me, always in heels, always in cute outfits and the kids absolutely adored her. I had wanted to strike up a friendship with her for ages but didn't know how or where to start without coming across like a weirdo.

She laughed as I scrambled onto my feet from my compromising position, and came further into my classroom, perching on the edge of a table.

'Sorry! I didn't mean to alarm you,' she said, still giggling. 'I just wanted to say well done. You were great in the meeting.' She spoke with such warm sincerity that I found myself welling up.

Even if she was disconcerted by my melodrama, I was grateful that she didn't show it. 'Listen, don't be so hard on yourself. That shit is not easy. You did really well. OK?'

I nodded, reluctantly. With that, Aurea got up and suddenly marched over to my grammar wall.

'I'm really sorry, but that has been annoying me since I came in here! How do you deal with your displays being so wonky?'

With no warning, she kicked off her stilettos and jumped on the table, taking out the drawing pins and straightening out the posters.

'I . . . um, I never noticed they were wonky,' I replied, meekly. 'I thought I did quite a good job, actually.' She turned and glared at me with mock disapproval and then proceeded to tug out more pins with exaggerated force. 'But . . . clearly not.' We both laughed.

As Aurea found more interior-designing work in my room, 'fixing' each display board that offended her, we chatted away. She told me about her life in Birmingham before she moved here, and I shared stories about my bonkers family. She filled me in on all the gossip about the other English teachers, like which teachers had applied for the Head of Department role but had been rejected, and were now harbouring a secret grudge. I didn't even notice the hours flying by until Mike popped in at 7 p.m. and told us it was time to lock up. At 7.30 p.m., we headed home, exhausted but euphoric. I remember thinking I had finally found a friend. I remember thinking I hadn't laughed like that in many months.

It felt so nice to have a laugh with someone who wasn't a child. All my life, I had been surrounded by friends. But then adulting took over and I metamorphosised into the flaky mate who never turned up or cancelled last minute. It says a lot about them that they continued to invite me. But at school, Aurea filled that void and became the friend that every girl needs: someone who would wait for me to go to lunch, someone who would tell me if I had a ladder in my tights and make me a cup of tea when I had a particularly hectic day. We formed quite a close friendship, and through her, I started socialising with other teachers too. Sometimes, she would even force me to sit in the English office, and would make an effort to bring me into the conversation. I usually messed it up by saying something cringeworthy or inappropriate or unfunny, but it was nice to have someone to laugh about it with after.

Aurea's assertiveness and spontaneity had another advantage as she decided overnight how important it was to get fresh air, and started dragging me out for walks around the school grounds.

'Right, Baigel. You're going for a walk,' she'd say, dragging me from my classroom every lunchtime. Somehow, we'd often find ourselves walking past the Hot Maths Teacher, playing football with the students on the Astroturf. I don't know when he ate lunch because whenever I saw him, he was with the kids. It was quite a lovely thing to see, actually, observing him and Mr Clarke (the married PE teacher who was 'banging' the Art teacher) laughing and joking with the boys who were desperately trying to impress them. Mr Clarke was much louder and more animated, play-fighting with the students and chanting insults in his victory anthems, whereas Mr Wilson was far more reserved, smiling at his mate's inappropriate conduct and keeping things under control.

Aurea told me they'd both been students at this school themselves, and I wondered if this was partly the reason why they were so dedicated to the children now. But as we walked around and I saw other teachers in action, I realised so many of them gave so much of themselves to the students out of genuine love, rather than any compulsion. They regularly came in during their holidays to teach additional classes, they worked overtime, and they did everything they could to support students. Obviously this commitment to the children was particularly attractive in the Hot Maths Teacher.

But when such a nurturing ethos is embedded within each fibre of the school, it is easy to blur the boundaries between work and life. And when you don't find the time to rest, your body chooses the time for you.

I was guiding my Year 8s through a particularly dry and pointless hour of leaflet design when I started to feel really unwell. I put it down to the fact that I hadn't eaten breakfast and was desperate for a wee. Maybe I was coming down with something, which wouldn't be surprising with so many little pathogens swarming around me all day, every day. Most teachers were frequently sick and I, in particular, permanently had the sniffles as my immune system hadn't become accustomed to the constant exposure to germs yet. Usually, I would ignore the symptoms and plod along, in sickness and in health. But that day, I stared at the clock, desperate for it to be lunchtime, and as soon as the bell rang and I could permissibly leave the students, rushed out of the classroom and straight into the toilet.

I took a couple of extra moments in there, head in my hands, just listening to the sound of my own breathing and enjoying the stillness of the air. I felt so weak that I could have easily had a nap, had I stayed one more second. As I got up to flush, however, I noticed that the toilet was filled with blood. Not just a little bit of spotting blood, but an alarming amount. It wasn't my time of the month, nowhere close . . . so what the fuck was that?

Of course, I was worried. But as Aurea rapped on the door for me to hurry up, I didn't have the time to dwell on it for too long. I loaded my knickers with some tissue and set off, breaking into a sprint when I remembered that it was my turn for lunch duty. I had to reach my spot before hundreds of children caused carnage and the woman in charge of the staff duty attendance blamed it all on me. Ms Hitcherson – or Ms Bitcherson, as named by the students, not me – didn't need an excuse to get me fired. Thankfully, by the time she came around with her register, I was standing in position by the school gates in the freezing cold, smiling sweetly, munching on some school fish and chips.

My bleeding continued for weeks and I started dreading going to the toilet. My vaginal issues weren't something I wanted to discuss with my colleagues; even though I had built good relationships with some of them, I didn't think we were close enough for me to disclose such intimate details. Female health is so undiscussed anyway, but at that age, in my early twenties, I definitely was embarrassed and didn't know enough about my own body to be able to talk about it comfortably. As for my family, I didn't want to worry them, as Dad acts like a sneeze is a declaration of a terminal illness. I felt completely alone and told no one. I had hoped that sweeping my symptoms under the carpet would make it all better, but nothing was getting better, and it was becoming harder and harder to keep the mask of calm intact, when underneath I was in chaos.

Throughout those weeks I didn't take a day off – it wasn't an option. Or at least, it didn't feel like it was. It was April, which meant the GCSE examinations were fast approaching and every free second of every day was filled with marking mocks, invigilating exams, or comforting stressed students. As well as adding to the workload of my colleagues, taking a day off would also mean adding to the anxiety of my students, who were typically trying to cram a two-year sylla-bus into the last two weeks. Aside from anything else, I knew that the process of being absent and setting cover would be far more draining than dragging my dying self into work. Teachers can't just call in sick and enjoy the rest of their day in bed. If I had taken a day off, I would have had to make sure every lesson was planned – with accompanying resources – and attached any instructions for the supply teacher. I would have had to call in every morning before 7.30 a.m. to inform the cover supervisor, which was always a really embarrassing phone call to make because you had to think of new, imaginative ways to make yourself sound acceptably sick over the phone. By the time I did all of that, I may as well have gone into school. So I did. Because it was so much easier to continue to pretend everything was fine, when it really, really wasn't.

It never rains but it pours, and when it pours in school it's a Monsoon. In the midst of my gynaecological nightmare, Ms Kowalski announced that we were going to be completing a 'marking scrutiny' at the end of the week. All teachers would be asked to bring exercise books from one class for senior leadership to scrutinise, so they could decide whether the marking met the school's expected standards or not. I can tell you now my marking didn't meet the standard . . . for the simple reason that I hadn't done any.

I was proud of how well my students were doing: I provided them with plenty of verbal feedback in the lesson and they were making fantastic progress, so this marking scrutiny felt like a total tick-box exercise. With all the balls I was juggling, and all the energy my students were bringing to class, some red pen on a piece of homework just didn't feel that important. But I didn't have the guts to say any of this. I was willing to sacrifice everything to try and submit something, had the powers that be told me which class, or which year group, was going to be checked. Of course, they deliberately withheld this crucial information. Nothing senior teachers love more than a cruel and merciless trap.

So it was that time again – time to call a cab and fill it up with seven large boxes, each one filled with thirty-two exercise books. I nearly cried on my way home at the thought of every book filled with reams and reams of writing, waiting to be corrected and commented on. I fantasised about throwing the boxes in the river (like the poor GCSE examiner in 2008 who threw 450 English scripts into the Thames because he couldn't meet the deadline) and making up some excuse about a mysterious theft. In the words of Jane Austen, 'Nothing can be compared to the misery of being bound to marking.' Well, Austen didn't say that exactly – but a slight adaptation reflects the plight of English teachers.

I knew this operation was never going to be accomplished alone. This had to be a family affair. Once my sister got home, exhausted from her own job, I begged her to help me. We decided on the strategy of marking two pieces in each book in detail, the others sparsely, and we recruited Mum to tick the blank pages. Ofsted had just introduced a new initiative called 'Response to Marking' where they wanted to see that the students had formally replied to their teacher's comments, creating a dialogue between student and teacher. So, at the end of the conveyor-belt marking process, each book came back to me, and I picked up a green pen and in my best student handwriting, wrote, 'Thanks Miss. I will try harder wit my spellingz' and similar variations in each book I marked. We did this all week, like a marking machine, working into the early hours. As a result, I was late to school – a few times actually – texting my co-tutor in a panic on my way in to cover form time. It was only by about five minutes but, in teaching, you aren't allowed to accidentally sleep in or have someone jump in front of your tube because it means putting thirty-two unsupervised children at risk. Nevertheless, despite all the extra effort, we still didn't finish.

I considered not going in on the day of the marking scrutiny and got numerous 'But you have to' lectures from my family. I told my mum I had a belly ache on the morning to which she reminded me that I was a teacher now and not a student, pulling off my blanket, just like she would when I was a teenager. By Friday morning, the Day of Judgement, I had worked myself up into an absolute state. I even wore flats. As I entered the faculty meeting, I had all my fingers and toes crossed that it would be my Year 10 or 11 books that would be collected. I had made the cunning assumption that the senior leadership team would be more concerned about GCSE classes, so had completed marking those. But of course, it was my Year 8 books that were summoned. With a broken heart, I handed my half-marked books in, and completed the walk of shame back to my classroom.

As I was wallowing in my misery, a bright and sparky Aurea bounced in and, in a replay of our initial meeting, stopped at the all-too-familiar sight of my quivering bottom lip. I knew my emotions were probably heightened from the lack of sleep, and I confessed between sobs that my books had entire pieces of work that hadn't been touched.

'Oh, honey . . .' She put a sympathetic arm around me. 'You should have just said that class has taken their books home, and offered one of the class sets that were marked.

That's what we always do.' I stared at her, stunned. How had that not even occurred to me? I had been so embarrassed to admit that I was falling behind, I never even thought that the other teachers were all feeling exactly the same. I imagined cupboards and desks stuffed with unmarked books. It was the great secret of the teaching profession – most teachers skip weeks of marking, let it pile up or don't do any at all. Sometimes they put a cursory tick and a mark and give it back, in case an overzealous parent sends in a complaint, but more often than not they'll just not return it at all. The truth is, many teachers had turned into Dorian Gray, with shameful secrets they didn't want revealed, not just me. I just hadn't known.

Aurea wiped a treacherous tear that had made its way down my cheek. 'Listen, go home, have a nice bath, get an early night, and come back with your heels on Monday. Because that . . .' she said, pointing at my Toms with a laugh, 'is totally unacceptable.'

I did go straight home and I did get an early night, but you know what they say: no amount of sleep will help when your soul is tired. I had even started planning lessons in my sleep, and falling asleep in lessons. It was a type of tiredness I can't explain – an utter state of mental, emotional and physical exhaustion. During my free periods, I locked my classroom from the inside, kept the key in the keyhole so no one could enter, turned the light off, and had naps in the corner of the room. I lay on a bean bag on the floor, using my coat as a blanket, and didn't wake up until the bell had gone. I had become prone to frequent migraines and was surviving by popping pills (Nurofen and paracetamol) every two hours, every single day. God knows what that was doing to my insides. Showering became a luxury and dry shampoo became my best friend. I finally decided to spice things up and give myself a four-day working week by falling sick every Wednesday, and that provided me with some level of respite – one day a week dedicated to recovery. But it didn't last long.

Soon after I took the executive decision to unofficially go part-time, I was pulled into Ms Kowalski's office, where she and Ms Bitcherson were waiting for me. I knew it was going to be a conversation about my marking – and that was the starting point. Apparently, Mrs Adjei had also complained about me and was 'concerned that Robbie was not getting sufficient support'. I wanted to tell them there and then about Mrs Adjei and her notes, but it would have looked defensive in response to her criticism and they would have asked why I hadn't mentioned it earlier. So I said nothing. The conversation moved on to my attendance and I nodded in agreement. My shame turned to disbelief, as they started reading out a list of all the heinous crimes I had committed since I joined. Apparently they were numerous, and terrible.

I was banned from having students in my class at break or lunch any more, because I was investing so much time into them that I was falling behind on the 'important' work. This progressed on to how 'some teachers were becoming irate because of how I was filling out the student report cards with numbers way higher than the students deserved'. (A report card was something especially reserved for naughty students which every teacher filled out after the lesson, in order for them to be monitored by their form tutors and heads of year. We would grade them on 1-5, 5 being amazing. I regularly awarded 5s to my students, because they were genuinely brilliant in my lessons.) But in summary, because of an accumulation of these offences, I was informed that I was being put on an Action Plan, where they would set me targets and every week, I would be reviewed by Ms Bitcherson – to cement the cruel irony of my life – to see if I was meeting them. And if I wasn't, I would lose my job.

I'm not being funny, and I understand my books weren't marked, but to make it seem like I wasn't teaching the kids well seemed completely unreasonable. In any other walk of life, a student doing well would be seen as a positive achievement, and worthy of praise, but it seemed like I was being punished for success. I wasn't on top of my marking, but my students *were* brilliant, and more importantly they were engaged, happy and confident. In one clean sweep, all my hard work and positive contributions were diminished. What about the fact that my GCSE classes last year had smashed their target grades by a mile? Or the money I spent out of my own underpaid pocket to buy the students adequate stationery? There were teachers shagging in the cupboards getting promoted and I was getting action-planned for being five minutes late to assembly? It was, frankly speaking, utter bullshit.

It was impossible not to feel disillusioned. No wonder that up and down the country, there were so many teachers battling drug and alcohol addictions, as a way of coping with the pressure of the job. The religious pub visits every Friday were more a desperate attempt to unwind from the traumas of that week, rather than a social. I didn't really see the point in working myself to the bone, when no one acknowledged it, no one commended it, no one nominated me for 'Colleague of the Bloody Week' and no one gave a shit about me, my wellbeing, or my health. Nobody cared, so why should I?

But I did, and we do, so I carried on. Just before the summer holiday, I was exiting the toilets after another bloody incident with shaking hands, and my worry must have been visible on my face because Ms Lewis noticed and pulled me straight into her office. All it took was for her to ask if I was OK, and I burst into tears, uncontrollably shaking and gasping for air between sobs. I explained what had been happening and she was horrified as she comforted me. I sat there, just sobbing and dribbling on her shoulder for a bit, and relishing someone consoling me for once. I had forgotten how lovely it was to be cared for – and how much relief there was in letting your guard down. Ms Lewis insisted that I went home immediately and I tried to resist, explaining that I was already on an Action Plan; I promised I would make a doctor's appointment as soon as the GCSE classes had left, but she was having none of it. She collected my bag and coat from my classroom so the kids wouldn't see the state of me and ordered me a cab home.

I was admitted into hospital the same day and, as I went through some important tests and examinations of my own, I realised what a fool I had been to leave it so late. It was only when I was lying in the hospital ward that I had the chance to reflect on the sacrifices we all had made in order to prioritise our jobs and students.

Of course we want to try our best for the students and give them as much as we can – and of course we should – but at what point does the balance tip and go from enough to too much? We are embarrassed to say that you shouldn't give your all because it makes us look less noble, like a less good teacher, selfish – but self-care is not selfish. And God, I wish I had learned that earlier. I wish I'd learned to say that I'll get done what I get done, and that's all I can do.

I worked in a faculty of twenty-five women and none of them were married. Some tried, and I saw them get married and divorced within a year. Some struggled with fertility issues; others had children they didn't get to spend any time with. Women, I feel, are particularly prone to giving too much of themselves, whilst accepting very little support in return. As working women, we feel like we have to continuously be strong and prove – to ourselves more than anyone else – that we don't need anyone to help us. We don't want to be dependent on anyone and view vulnerability as a weakness. We push ourselves beyond what our bodies permit and only realise how much life passed us by after it is too late. But you have to look after yourself – because no one else is going to do it for you.

No one will congratulate you for missing your daughter's Sports Day or your son's assembly or your best friend's wedding. All it will do is breed resentment. I remember how many family events I either missed or took my laptop or books of marking to. We're all so focused on trying to make a better life for others that we forget to enjoy the life we have. I'm not saying that I regret what I did for my school and my students, because I don't, but I do regret those moments I either missed or didn't make the most of. No one lies on their deathbed and wishes they'd worked more.

I spent so many years believing the world would stop if I took a single minute out, pressed the pause button or booked an appointment – but it didn't and it won't. The truth is that we are disposable, whether we like it or not. Life will continue, even without us, and the bell will ring again, but this time someone else will be running around in our place.

I always waited for the right time. It would be a good time once the GCSE exams were over; it would be a good time once the coursework had been moderated. But there is never a perfect time. Something will always be in the way. Life will always throw another excuse at you. Ultimately, you have to choose the moment and make it the perfect time.

Otherwise, this wonderful, rewarding, noble profession is unsustainable. Lying in that hospital bed, alone and terrified, I knew that I needed to nourish, nurture and protect my body in order to survive this journey.

And once I had understood and accepted this lesson, it made it easier to help others too.

4

Look After Each Other

My childhood in Tottenham gave me some of the best memories of my life. I think back to the five of us stacked on top of each other having singing competitions and watching Bollywood films on a ten-inch television screen. I remember when Mum and Dad fancied giving us a 'treat', they bought fish and chips and cut one cod into five small pieces for us all to share and savour. I kid you not, for me, no Michelin-star restaurant could provide the same satisfaction. This was the only life we knew, where excitement wasn't a skiing trip in the Alps, but rollerblading down to the corner shop with our mates and buying penny sweets. We weren't rich, but we didn't know any different life – we didn't know any better – and we were happy.

Yet when I tell people I taught at a secondary school in Tottenham, the usual reaction is for them to gasp in horror. Next, they tell me how brave I am, offering some variation of how 'they couldn't do it', quickly followed by an excited request to share any outrageous tales of bad behaviour. Expecting an episode of *Top Boy*, they are somewhat surprised and a tad disappointed when I tell them that I adored the extraordinary kids I taught.

I don't use the word 'extraordinary' lightly. I have met so many different kinds of people throughout my life: I have been fortunate enough to travel around the world and mix with people from all walks of life. And whilst each interaction has contributed to my personal growth, it was the invaluable time I spent with my students that completely changed me as a person.

The dichotomy between how my students are perceived by others versus the reality of their lives has been a constant challenge. Even now, I have to bite my tongue when I hear people spout their views about what they think my students must have been like and how I must have felt. Watching my kids ripped to shreds by media stereotypes and ignorant assumptions, knowing what I know, is difficult to tolerate.

I have endless memories of joyful teenage extravagance or weird and hilarious mishaps. There were the prom nights when the students turned up looking like A–list celebrities after months of slogging through exams. As the DJ took us through a playlist of grime, Bollywood and Turkish music, we all danced together until midnight. There were the trips to Thorpe Park, where I was shitting bricks but was practically bullied by my students into sitting on the most terrifying rides. And there was the time we were all caught doing the electric slide during an English lesson by the headteacher, who happened to be taking a visitor for a tour around the school in order to convince him for extra funding. Those memories will always hold a special place in my heart. But at the time, we didn't realise we were making memories. We just knew we were having fun.

It's actually some of the brief encounters and fleeting conversations that left a lasting impression on me and made me re-evaluate everything I thought I knew. My students believed that I was the fountain of knowledge, but I learned so much more from them – often in the most unexpected ways. Many of them had challenging lives – but what shone through was not their suffering but their resilience.

I knew that school was their escapism – and I'd had many calls with parents that showed me how tough some kids had it. To be honest, in those first few years, I was so focused on what was happening in the classroom, I didn't give proper attention to what was happening when the kids got home. Although I had seen their vulnerabilities and insecurities, often in one-to-one conversations, for the most part, they seemed so full of life, hurling insults, cracking jokes and shouting over each other. They put on a front, bringing a persona into school to impress their friends, and in my naivete, I assumed this meant that everything was okay when they left too.

As my inexperience evolved into a slight command of the classroom and I was finally able to stop worrying about myself, I had time to really open my eyes and look at the kids in front of me as people rather than puppets, with real and complex lives. A few encounters showed me that sometimes children are dealing with problems just as complex, stressful and all-consuming as any adult – and sometimes much worse. And in those moments, I started to feel more like an adult myself, a role I didn't realise I was growing into, so at least I could somewhat share the burden.

I didn't tell my students off very often, and can count the number of times I had to raise my voice on one hand, and that's probably why one incident remains etched in my memory. It began in a light-hearted, uneventful manner. I was doing my break duty one day and Mr Wilson was floating around me, eating some hot wings. I was in the middle of eyeing him up, but he must have misunderstood, and offered me some. Politely, I declined, and he left. Jackie, who had been snooping throughout the whole situation, said, 'You should take the wings, girl! You need to fatten up!' and I laughed, secretly thanking God that she had waited for Mr Wilson to leave before offering me this profound advice.

Just as my duty was about to end, a Year 9 girl, who I had never really come across before, dropped a dirty tissue on the canteen floor and then completely ignored it. I went up to her and asked her to pick it up, to which she replied, 'It's not my job.' I was taken aback. It was my first direct confrontation with a child and I didn't want the situation to escalate, so maintaining my composure, I smiled and asked her again, 'Darling, you dropped your dirty tissue, so you need to pick it up. Now, please.'

She literally looked me in my face and said, 'I'm not picking up the tissue. What are you going to do about it?' And with that, she kissed her teeth and walked off, laughing with her friends.

Abdullah, who was queuing for food, left the line, shouting to Ugur to keep his place, and rushed towards me.

'Are you OK, Miss? I'll pick up the tissue,' he said. I smiled despite the anger that was building up inside me.

'Don't worry about it, sweetheart. I'll handle it,' I said.

It was such a petty incident – my friend once was called a 'fat slag' by one of her students and another colleague was spat on, so this was hardly the biggest offence in the teacher world. I didn't actually care about the tissue, but it was more a matter of principle than anything else. She couldn't get away with refusing to follow instructions and speaking to me like that without any consequences, especially in front of other students. I had learned from my error of being too lenient in the past and therefore had to ensure that I dealt with this firmly.

So, I found out from another student that the girl's name was Ayce and went straight onto the computer system to find her home number and call her mum. I tried a few times, but no one picked up the phone. Frustrated, I went to the behaviour mentor, Joe, and recounted the lunchtime incident, but he didn't seem surprised. 'Her mum can't speak English, Miss. I know her well. Just tell me the details and I'll speak to Ayce myself.' I was worried that wouldn't have the same effect as informing her family, but I left it in his capable hands and made a mental note to chase it the next day.

As it turned out, Joe did what he had promised and the next day, Ayce came to my classroom and reluctantly apologised. It was decided that she had to spend the rest of the day in the duty room, where she was isolated from her peers for the entire day, including break and lunch. I was quite pleased with the outcome and the case was closed.

A couple of weeks later, I was unwell – again – and ended up in A&E late on a school night. I was already dreading going into work the next day because I wasn't allowed any more absences under the Action Plan. The school had been supportive and covered my lessons whilst I was away without me having to phone at 7.30 a.m. from the hospital bed, but that threat was still looming daily above my ailing body like a dark cloud and the stress of it created a circular loop of illness and recovery.

Whilst I was in the queue for Outpatients, waiting for my turn to sign in, I recognised the young girl who was just in front of me. It was Ayce, still in her school uniform and standing next to a woman in a wheelchair. As Ayce spoke to the receptionist, her mum, clearly distressed, repeatedly shouted and hit her daughter's arm. Every now and then, Ayce looked towards her mother and said something reassuring in Turkish, presumably explaining that there wasn't long left to wait now, and then turned back to the receptionist to finish providing the necessary information. I overheard her describe her mother's incontinence, saying she had changed her mother's clothes but brought the stained clothes with her in a bag, in case the doctor wanted to have a look. She was so calm as she went through the details – this fourteen-year-old girl – handling the entire situation with complete proficiency, as if it was a regular occurrence.

I felt like I was looking at a completely different girl to the one in the canteen. It was when they turned to walk towards the waiting area that Ayce noticed me. She waved excitedly – 'Hi, Miss!' – with no sign of a grudge or embarrassment, and as I smiled and waved back, she headed off to find a seat for the four-hour wait ahead of her.

Suddenly, the tissue incident seemed so futile and irrelevant. There I was worrying about going to work the next morning with a lack of sleep, and yet this girl was having to do repeated all-nighters in the hospital and just taking it all in her stride. All I had seen was a deliberate act of defiance; it didn't matter what else might be going on in this child's life. The coincidental insight into her personal context made me see the situation in a whole new light. I guess saying no to picking up the tissue was an element of her life where she could have some control, and where she had the power to say 'no'.

Seeing Ayce in the hospital made me think twice before making assumptions about my students. The knowledge that they might have bigger problems than I could imagine didn't mean that I excused bad behaviour or justified it, but it did mean that I was a little more careful, and didn't go barging in all guns blazing, every time I perceived what seemed to be disobedience. I paused. I took my time. I talked to the kids and searched for context. I wanted to know why. I learned to be aware of my position, and what I could do to support my students. That meant all my students, because it wasn't just the badly behaved or underperforming students who were dealing with a lot – even the star pupils were often under pressure.

Martyna in my Year 10 class, who did not speak a word of English only a couple of years ago, had not only managed to grasp the language but was now outperforming the majority of the native speakers. She was remarkably intelligent, incredibly conscientious and had high expectations of herself. This made it even more surprising that when I was checking the homework of my class at the start of one lesson – like I did every lesson – it was Martyna who said she hadn't done it. I was surprised but let her off the first time; however, the next time she missed the deadline, I kept her behind to speak to her.

She seemed uncomfortable, which was understandable as she wasn't used to being in trouble. She bit her bottom lip nervously and, once the last class member had left, spoke first. 'I'm sorry I didn't do my homework, Miss,' she said, looking directly at me, almost as if she was trying to gauge how angry I was. I sighed and sat at my desk.

'Martyna, it's not about being sorry. You not doing your homework doesn't affect me. It affects you. This is about your GCSEs – not mine.'

My voice was firm, and I didn't try to soften it. I had enough to worry about without my good students slipping through my fingers too. I also knew what Martyna was capable of, and after all her hard work, it was frustrating to watch her performance slip like this.

Martyna nodded but didn't respond. I waited for an excuse, but none came, so I continued.

'Completing your homework is vital for your revision, Martyna. I set it specifically so older topics stay fresh in your mind while we move ahead in class. You're in Year 10 now. This is not the time to get complacent.'

Martyna remained silent, still offering no excuse or explanation.

'Do you have anything to say?' I asked.

She shook her head. It was unlike her, and we both sat listening to the silence. I could no longer tell whether she was sad or exhausted or irritated. She was reluctant to talk, and I was reluctant to let it go.

'Did you not understand the homework task?' I asked. She shook her head. 'Did you have too much homework from other lessons?' She shook her head again. I sighed. 'Martyna, I can't help you if I don't know what's going on.'

There was another moment of silence, and I thought I would have to give in and move on, but then, after a slight hesitation, Martyna spoke.

'I didn't have time, Miss.'

I stared at her, unsure of what to make of this. I expected a more elaborate explanation – something more serious or more dramatic.

'You didn't have time?' I replied. She nodded. I waited.

'I had to pick up my brother after school, and then when we got home, I had to cook dinner for us.'

'Where was your mum?' I gently probed.

'She works until late, Miss. She doesn't get home until after my brother goes to bed.' I stayed quiet, and she continued to speak. 'I have to do my brother's homework with him and give him a bath before I put him to bed. It doesn't usually take that long but this week he had to create a volcano, so it took a long time.' She waited again. 'I tried to do my homework at 8.30 when he was in bed, but I was too tired, Miss. I had been up since 5.30.'

The picture began unravelling. 'I'm sorry if I sounded angry earlier,' I said. 'We can always catch up on any work you miss together before school, at lunchtime, or whenever you want to.'

She fidgeted with the cusp of her school jumper.

'I usually catch up on my work in the morning, but recently . . . I haven't been able to.'

'Why not?'

'My mum works in the morning. I help her . . . clean toilets and stuff in the morning before I come to school.'

People often say children need to 'work harder' – and I wonder how much harder they expect someone like Martyna to work. Martyna didn't want pity; she wanted to succeed and make life just a little bit easier for herself and her family. She wanted to help her mother, and was fiercely adamant that their challenging circumstances would not impact her little brother's future.

I don't know if I would have been able to persevere through the same battles as Martyna when I was fourteen, but after listening to her, I knew that if she could keep going every day with a smile on her face, I could definitely cope with the early starts and the excessive workload. In the course of that conversation with Martyna, I knew I had to learn to manage with the stress, the Action Plan and the complete lack of work–life balance, if it meant making life a bit easier for children like her. It was a reminder of why I signed up in the first place and for the first time in a long time, I felt my cynicism was overtaken by a strange sensation, like an unused muscle had been brought into action once again. More than anything else, it was a reminder that a school is a support system, a network that everyone is a part of and I had to ensure I upheld my part in that network.

It was many years after this, during the pandemic, that Marcus Rashford emerged as a champion for children and began his campaign to bring a conversation about child poverty into the public domain. People finally got a glimpse of the reality of child hunger that had been brutally clear in schools for years. We would see children putting rolls in their pockets at lunch, or asking for a bit of someone else's homemade sandwich at break. More often it was clear in their disengagement during lessons all morning, the desperate run as soon as the lunch bell went, or in their visible lethargy caused by a cheap, unhealthy diet.

But as teachers, there was very little we could do. We couldn't reach out to the parents, we couldn't send a weekly grocery shop to their house and we certainly couldn't take them home for a hot meal. For the most part, we just had to hope the cafeteria staff loaded them up. But when I saw it in my own classroom, I tried to help on a smaller scale, to at least do *something*. I noticed Ceylan's hunger for the first time during a silent poetry assessment. Her belly started rumbling loudly and as the class broke into giggles, I jokingly told them I thought it was mine. I knew how embarrassing this would be for any child, let alone a girl who didn't like any attention on her. To divert the attention away from Ceylan, I began to share deliberately outrageous anecdotes of my belly rumbling like an earthquake during the most inappropriate times like during interviews and hot dates. A chorus of 'Me too!' erupted around the class.

After the lesson, I kept Ceylan behind and offered to have lunch together. She seemed wary but agreed and I ordered us two meals from the local Turkish restaurant. As we waited for the food to arrive, I chatted away and casually asked her what she had eaten for breakfast. She paused, looking at me as if she were trying to figure out whether I could be trusted, before it all just tumbled out. She said she hadn't eaten anything for breakfast, nor had she eaten any dinner the night before, because there wasn't any food in the house and there was no adult around to go and buy some. Ceylan was the eldest child in her family, with three younger siblings. Her mother had suddenly passed away when she was in Year 7 and her father, already working ridiculous night shifts, was struggling to cope with the additional responsibility of trying to look after the children that she had left behind. This meant that he spent any rare hours at home locked away in his bedroom, unable to face them, and didn't always remember to buy the groceries. Ceylan's dream was to get to university because that would make her one step closer to becoming independent, and in doing so, she would be able to lessen her father's worries.

She tore chunks out of the bread as she spoke and her eyes were welling up. I didn't want to press her further so I changed the subject, no doubt to something completely inane like television. It was the thirteen-year-old girl who brought the conversation back to something important: her faith. It still amazes me that some of my students retained their strong belief in religion and never faltered at the hardships they endured. It is so easy to become cynical and blame religion when it doesn't have the answers – in my experience, it is a common thing for adults to do – but in the case of some of these children, they found that praying helped them cope with their ordeals. It was in that conversation that Ceylan first invited me to attend the Friday Muslim prayers held in the Dance Hall each week.

Our school accommodated all faiths with a complete commitment to inclusivity and tolerance. I'll never forget the first time I stepped into the hall with her: it was filled with students from all year groups, all from diverse backgrounds, greeting each other and working together to lay out the mats, despite never speaking to each other outside of that hall. Some tiny, Year 7 latecomers sneaked in and made their way to the back row, and giant Year 11s shuffled over to make some space for them. They stood there, shoulder to shoulder with teachers, coordinated in a wave of perfectly synchronised movements.

Mr Azad, from the Science department, sat at the front and first delivered a sermon, telling a story about the importance of speaking to each other with kindness. We all listened intently, as he linked the Islamic values of respect and tolerance with the school's. To my surprise, even Mr Thorne popped down to visit, but he wasn't exactly sure about how the rules worked; he took off his shoes and kneeled next to the female row, whispering 'This is fantastic', unaware that he was supposed to be silent and with the boys. I watched as the student next to him quietly whispered what he should be doing and he tried to be inconspicuous as he moved to the correct row. The boys shuffled aside, making space for him.

At the end of the prayer, all the students tidied up together, putting away the mats and making sure that the hall looked exactly as when we came in. The teachers, including me, handed out some juice and pizza for the kids as they made their way out of the hall, back into the world.

It was such a magical break from the madness of school: in that hall, just for a few minutes, everything stopped. There was no 'popular' student and no school hierarchy and no noise. Just a hall filled with people praying for the change they wanted to see. And I understood exactly why Ceylan found inner peace there.

Ceylan and I started having lunch regularly, and I also arranged a homework session twice a week after school. With pizza. It wasn't much of course, but it gave her some small moments of support while her Head of Year worked to support her father. I started praying with my students regularly and those moments offered me time to think and reflect and unwind. They also gave me comfort from the constant intensities I was experiencing. Nothing in my training had prepared me to deal with the daily suffering of children and the variety of individual experiences. What were you supposed to do when a student fell asleep in class because the police had raided their house at 2 a.m. the night before? What was the right thing to say to a child who had just been taken into care and separated from their sibling? No one trained me on how to console children who suffered from bereavement, or how to offer them hope when they were diagnosed with a terminal illness. As a teacher, I lived in a polarised world of extreme emotions, where within a single day, I cried both tears of laughter as well as pain. But in the words of Charles Dickens, 'No one is useless in schools who lightens the burden of another.' Well, he didn't say 'in schools' but I think you get the sentiment. All I could do, and tried to do, was share their pain and offer support where I could.

Nowadays, I hear young people being labelled as 'snow-flakes'. I hear people talking about how children should be more resilient. And I think it's utterly laughable. Until people in privileged positions actually spend time with these kids and their families, they cannot even begin to comprehend what the reality is like for so many young people growing up in Britain today. And if they were put in the children's shoes for just a week, I guarantee, they wouldn't even last a second.

Yet these students persevere. With all that's going on in their lives, it's an achievement many of them even make it to school in the first place. But they do. They come to school every day and they try to concentrate, with empty stomachs and broken homes and more responsibility resting on their little shoulders than they should ever be asked to carry.

I contrast their perseverance against all adversities with other children from privileged backgrounds. I used to think that they only have to sneeze before being diagnosed with an allergy to sunlight and getting millions of advantages as a result. Sometimes I hear of stories my friends and family tell me of school refusers, children who are clinically being treated for depression, on heavy medication, because 'their parents don't understand them'. And I think perhaps money brings more problems than it eases. I do understand that wealthy children may suffer from their own issues – addict parents or workaholics who have left their children to be raised by nannies – leading to a series of problems of their own. Absent fathers are just as bad as fathers who fly off with their new girlfriend, leaving their fourteen-year-old in charge of younger siblings with access to his credit card for meals. But one thing I learnt from training in a grammar school is that privilege may not prevent suffering, but provides resources which affect how these issues are dealt with. My students didn't have the money for diagnoses and treatment plans and therapists – the irony of all this being, perhaps they're the ones who deserved them the most – and they learned to live without. I believe that the work ethic that I maintain today is inspired by the students I taught. My students shaped the way I view the world, by teaching me to not fixate on my problems and keep moving forward no matter how difficult the time.

It was within this dynamic that the interconnectedness of human experience became much more profound for me. We were all impacting one another consciously and subconsciously, and the ethos of our school, of us all being a family, reinforced that even more. The way my school was structured created a sense that we were all in this together and therefore had to look after each other. Sometimes that structure failed, and James's exclusion taught me to never rely on that network of protection. Then of course, sometimes it was overbearing, and my Action Plan wasn't soon forgotten. But for the most part, this nurturing and supportive environment helped the children to blossom and also allowed me to grow. The fact that we had students who had completed their education but still came back years later to visit their teachers is a powerful testimony to what can be done when you genuinely create a school embedded in love and care.

And little did I know, love was finally finding a way into my life too. On a cold winter afternoon, after the particularly draining confrontation involving that young girl and a tissue, I got back to my table and saw a pot of hot wings left on it with one of my pink Post-it notes stuck to it, which simply said, 'Enjoy x'.

5

Girls Need Feminism in Many Forms

Now you may think that my negative experience with my cheating ex is the reason why I'm still unmarried ten years later. But that's not the case. It's not that I'm against men, or marriage, or anything like that, but that unfortunate courtship simply made me much more aware of the qualities I actually needed in a partner: loyalty, respect, and maybe I'm asking for too much here, but someone who doesn't believe women should be locked away in the house . . . that sort of thing.

I didn't really understand the importance of feminism until I started teaching and can't pinpoint what exactly sparked my initial awakening to all its forms. It's something I'm quite ashamed to admit, but until my mid-twenties, I never even thought about gender equality or considered my role in the world as a woman. My life as a young adult was basically spent flitting between writing essays and thinking of the next excuse to sneak out of the house with my friends, and my knowledge of the wider world was very limited beyond that. Having attended two girls' schools myself, I thought I was pretty clued up about many of the problems

I'd have to deal with – and some were the same, because friendship dilemmas and heartbreaks and eating disorders continue to rear their ugly heads throughout the different generations. And I am still no expert, but working with hundreds of teenage girls meant I was immersed in the trials and tribulations of their lives, and I had to learn to deal with their issues sensitively, fairly and firmly.

The beauty of literature is that you can create an environment of discussion and debate through fictional characters and scenarios without targeting any specific individuals, and that allows us to apply these concepts to our own lives. *Oliver Twist* could be used to discuss class and crime, *The Hate U Give* allowed us to explore police brutality and racism, whilst *Dr Jekyll and Mr Hyde* provided the perfect access to talk about homosexuality. When I was teaching *The Taming of the Shrew* to my Year 8 class, as an introduction to the themes in the play, I asked my students to put their hands up if they considered themselves feminists. Not a single student raised their hand. I was surprised by their unanimous disdain; I am not saying I was expecting all of them to declare their affiliation to the suffrage movement, but I was at least expecting some kind of debate that would take up the rest of the lesson. Their reasons for rejecting feminism varied. Gulsen admitted she didn't know what the word meant, and many others agreed with her. Amisha tried to explain it to them, saying it was 'the women who hate men'. Ugur then tipped me over the edge by offering his own definition of feminists: 'the women who are bare hairy'. After that description and the eruption of laughter that followed, even the students who were considering joining the dark side were too embarrassed to admit it.

When the lesson was over, I went straight into Aurea's classroom to vent about my students' disappointing reaction; she giggled as I re-created my desperate attempt to evoke some sort of passion out of them, along with a re-enactment of the students' utter boredom and derision. Smugly, Aurea declared that she felt confident she would get a better reaction out of her own class and we made a bet for her to test it out on them the following lesson. However, she had to come off her high horse quite quickly, as the very next day, she confessed that her students had responded in exactly the same way as mine.

We carried this discussion to the English office, and as some other teachers began to share their views, it became clear that we definitely weren't all on the same page. My students didn't know what feminism was, but I started to think most of us weren't really sure either. Ms Bloome was appalled by the reaction of the students, even suggesting that we revisit all the texts we study in English to expose them to political topics right from Year 7, and Ms Kowalski nodded in agreement. But then Mrs Haider joined in and said she agreed with the students, because she didn't feel like the feminist movement spoke to her or for her in any way. They continued discussing racial erasure and white privilege and things got very heated, particularly when Holly, who I was getting to know quite well, said that it was 'a movement made by white women for white women and many of our students were right to feel alienated by it'. I kept quiet because I didn't have the same level of facts and knowledge that they had. But I was interested. I had never considered the race aspect to this debate before and as a woman of colour myself, I was just swaying somewhere in the middle, listening to everyone's viewpoints and trying to determine my own. When I'd asked the question, I'd expected a united front in response to the children's confusion, but instead it felt like I'd asked if they believed in aliens – and this was in a room filled with strong, professional women. In that moment, I had regressed into being a student again, trying to figure out my political identity and not getting anywhere fast.

This meant I had as much to learn as my class as we worked through the rest of the play. The importance of facilitating open and honest conversations around gender roles, patriarchy, sexual harassment and representation became very apparent. At first, it seemed like all the girls in the class were in agreement. As we explored and analysed Petruchio's objectification of Kate, many of the girls were appalled and said they would never let a man dictate their life in that way.

'Why does he think he can run up in here and change everything about her?' Leyla asked. 'Did he buy her?'

Most of the girls nodded in agreement.

'If someone tried to do that to me, I swear I would not have it,' Tegan added. 'I'm not a servant.'

But when the scene had finished, Amisha, who had been listening intently, put her hand up.

'I don't see why we're acting like Petruchio did something wrong,' she said. 'Kate clearly had anger issues, and he made her a better person. There's nothing wrong with that.'

There was an excited response – a chatter between the students on their tables – and there were some back and forth retorts between those who agreed with Amisha and those who were outraged.

'So men can have opinions but women can't? Women should just be housewives?' Tegan said.

'I'm not saying that. I'm just saying that there is nothing wrong with serving your husband,' Amisha replied.

There was an immediate outcry in response to the word 'serving', and in a blink of an eye, a stream of hands shot up in the air.

'Being a housewife doesn't make you weak,' Ojani came in, offering fierce defence of her friend. 'My grandma was a housewife. She considered my granddad to be the head of the household. But she's still the strongest woman I know.'

'It's her duty to be a better wife. My mum cooks for my dad when he gets home from work and that makes her happy,' said Amisha.

'If that's what women want to do, that's their business,' Leyla replied. 'I'm not serving anyone.'

What 'empowerment' and 'aspiration' looked like for these girls varied dramatically according to their upbringing. There was no right or wrong answer. Of course I understood what Leyla and Tegan were saying and admired the comfort and ease with which they recognised their own value – but Amisha's view wasn't wrong either. One of the issues with feminism is that the attack against subservience comes from a one-dimensional social construct of power, understood in one culture, that isn't applicable to the rest of the world, with all of its many cultural nuances. As the western world moves forward with its feminist ideas, it dismisses traditional values and labels them as 'oppressive'. And as the students debated with each other and sometimes even with me, my own views evolved with theirs.

It was not always easy to maintain neutrality, and sometimes the complexity of working with communities who didn't see the value of educating women was definitely tricky – though I didn't come across this often. During my teaching career, I did encounter girls who expressed that they would get married soon after they completed their secondary education, like Sara who said she was 'being taken back home to get married straight after GCSEs'. These ideologies made it difficult to motivate girls to work hard at school and see the benefits of gaining qualifications, and we had to work carefully with them and their families to try and understand the protection an education could give them, even after marriage. Those conversations required a great deal of sensitivity, because enforcing our opinions onto the families wouldn't have achieved anything but hostility and conflict. It was crucial to work with the communities we were based in, not against them.

I had come across these attitudes often enough in my own personal life, where my friends, who, despite being bright, talented and full of potential, had their hearts set on searching for rich and successful husbands who could support and provide for them. Distant relatives often told – and still tell – my family that they should have married me off in my early twenties, and that excessive focus on my career as a female would not be advisable. My so-called 'independence' (despite me still living at home at twenty-five, and having a stricter curfew than my Year 8s) was not just off-putting for potential suitors, but also for my students' parents. It was tricky, because I knew that when I met some parents to talk about their daughters, they would disapprove of me – the way I dressed, or looked, or acted – because I was a woman who they would interpret to be 'too modern'. I embodied everything they actively discouraged their daughters from becoming and therefore they would be wary of what I had to say. But I did understand some parents' fear of their daughters losing their traditional, cultural or religious values

– my own parents were desperate to hold on to their heritage and feared us becoming 'too Westernised', whilst our cousins back home were losing their virginities in the toilets of LUMS University. It was a delicate balance and one I tried my best not to upset.

I attended a meeting with Sara's parents and explained that I wasn't trying to make their daughter stray from the 'right path' and that I wasn't a 'bad influence'. I just wanted to ensure that she had an education to fall back on if, for any reason, her marriage didn't work out, or even if her husband needed support himself. Her dad wasn't too convinced, but I could see that Sara's mum appreciated where I was coming from, though she didn't say anything. We talked about the dangers of financial dependency and how this could lead to women being controlled by their partners, and the fact that education could give their daughters a real sense of freedom and security. Whatever they decided to go and do in the future, it was my job to prepare them to make informed decisions. For me, autonomy and the right to choose were synonymous with female empowerment.

This helped me regain some of the confidence I had lost since I started teaching. I'll be the first to admit that my journey thus far wasn't perfect, and I certainly wasn't perfect. I made countless mistakes over the first few years, and I let myself tumble into despair or distress. But at the same time, I kept it together in the classroom and many of my students flourished, surpassing their target grades by a mile. But there is something unique about being a young woman in this world – particularly one in her early twenties. If in fifty cases, we experience forty-nine praises and one criticism, we tend to only fixate on the single negative comment and ignore the forty-nine successes – any excuse to self-depre-cate. And even if we were proud of our achievements, we would stop ourselves from shouting from the rooftops because we wouldn't want to look narcissistic, or arrogant, or vain. And I was no different.

The worst thing about not being a cheerleader for myself is that no one else would take up the role either. I had no defence, or dissenting voice, against the subtle digs or more explicit sneers, and it had eaten away at me. It felt like it was considered impossible that my students were making progress because I was working really, really hard or because maybe . . . just maybe . . . I was actually quite good at what I did. From the moment my own father asked if I was going to a 'fashion show' on my first day, I got comments on my appearance, and a total disregard for my ability. I'll never forget when Mr Lever wondered aloud whether my obser-vation was 'outstanding' because the boys 'had hard-ons under the desk'. From being one of the highest achievers in every institution I had been in, I had suddenly been reduced to nothing more than a little girl with bright nails and hair extensions, and I had never been made to feel so worthless.

This constant diminishing of my abilities made me doubt myself and what I had to offer, and whilst the students looked up to me for guidance and direction, I lost the cour-age to speak up in meetings for fear of being mocked or dismissed. Often, I played up to the part, dumbing myself down and speaking in a soft voice, because that was easier than trying to prove I was good enough. Every other day, a teacher would ask how I could walk in heels, or pass some comment about my make-up. And it wasn't just the male teachers. Once, when I went to thank Ms Bitcherson for a training session (and offer an olive branch), she looked me up and down, and said, 'Oh, look. The Post-its match your lipstick.'

But people discredit you in order to compensate for their own feelings of inadequacy. In my experience, women sniggered, whilst men sexualised. There were clear parallels between the way female staff and students were treated; in the same way that the boys would think it was acceptable to smack the bums of girls wearing shorter skirts, female teachers were frequently belittled and demeaned in the name of 'banter'. And this culture of everyday sexism was, and is, constantly overlooked in schools.

Even though I still hadn't figured out my brand of feminism, I knew one thing for sure – I wasn't interested in the kind that looks down on women who live their lives in a way that doesn't adhere to society's rigid expectations. Perhaps that's why I reacted particularly badly to the International Women's Day assembly that year.

It was supposed to be a massive celebration of womanhood – a ground-breaking event in which teachers were going to candidly reveal their own experiences as women and award prizes to female students who had demonstrated exceptional courage and determination. To add to the significance of the occasion, the first period of the day had been cancelled and external guests had been invited. All the girls were given an 'I AM STRONG' badge to wear as they entered the hall and you could tell that they were finally eager to be included in an event that was putting women at the forefront. I wore my badge with pride.

Two female members of staff, one History teacher and one Biology, stepped onto the stage and hugged each other. It was a cute way to open and immediately gave positive vibes. We all cheered as they moved towards the podium. 'Good morning, everyone ... and Happy INTERNATIONAL WOMEN'S DAY!' Ms Manning, the History teacher, shouted into the mic, and the crowd responded with more applause. It was like watching a concert. The girls needed this – some motivation, and dedicated time to remind them of their self-worth, and there was a strong sense of sisterhood.

'Now ... a lot of you girls like getting long eyelashes, or like these long, false nails,' Ms Manning continued with creepy-crawly hand gestures. 'But if you want to be taken seriously, it is so important that you don't waste your time, your money and your energy on these ... pointless, pointy things. Isn't that right, Miss?' She jovially nudged her partner, Ms Hall, who nodded animatedly in agreement. From across the hall, Aurea looked at me and rolled her eyes.

'Absolutely, Miss! How do you see through those awful lashes anyway?' As she made a dramatic gesture of blindness in an attempt at humour, there were barely any laughs. I saw every girl around that hall who needed empowering the most visibly switch off. Some students turned to look at me, disappointed. I had to disguise my own because what else could I do?

It was clear that this was not a celebration of being female at all. It was, in fact, just another group of women projecting a very fixed and narrow version of how they expected progressive women to look and act and dress and behave and be. Although I understood the purpose of what the teachers were trying to achieve, their approach and method felt wrong. Telling girls to let go of all the things they love and enjoy – all the things that are seen as cool, as desirable – wasn't the answer. And as I watched a sea of girls with hair extensions, fake nails and different priorities tune out, I couldn't help but feel that this was a completely wasted opportunity.

I applauded reluctantly with my fake nails and gave a standing ovation on my very high heels, and I couldn't help feeling complicit in the indoctrination of the myth that, somehow, feminism and femininity were mutually exclusive.

Whilst women were increasingly glamourised in the media, I saw so many girls turning away from education because they felt they had to make a choice between what kind of girl they wanted to be – the Malala or the Kylie Jenner. This ideology of women being either pretty or intelligent was not anything new – we read books in our childhood like *Matilda*, in which we were taught that women could either 'choose looks, or choose books'. But what we should have been doing was encouraging our students to enjoy their own interests, whilst helping them understand that their appearance is just one aspect of the immeasurable qualities that make up their identity.

We all piled into the staffroom immediately after the assembly to make frantic cups of coffee before our first lessons, whilst providing a quick post-mortem of what was witnessed on stage. Aurea was in a fit of giggles, whilst Ms Bloome tried to be more empathetic towards the two teachers, adding, 'Their intentions were good – but God almighty, their execution left a lot to be desired!'

Before I could say what I was thinking, Mrs Adjei, who had been sitting doing a crossword, looked up.

'There was nothing wrong with what they were saying,' she said. 'Nowadays, girls have nothing to offer except their looks.' And with a final glare towards me, she walked out of the staffroom, leaving me to try and avoid Ms Bloome's embarrassed glances in my direction.

Jackie, who was filling up the fridge with milk, passed me the carton I was reaching for. 'Did you win Woman of the Year?' she said, and I couldn't help but smile.

'Not this time, Jackie,' I shrugged. 'Maybe next year.' She patted me on my back and walked off shaking her head, no doubt making a mental note to give me a second helping at lunch.

In the classroom, girls swarmed me saying 'what a waste of time' the assembly had been and I remained professional, trying to find meaning and value in what could only be described as a shitshow. I looked at my girls and considered how they were often dismissed, or cast in a different light because their spirit was seen as 'attitude' as compared to the more acceptable 'laddish' energy of boys. I sometimes felt like some teachers would rather extinguish the fire in the girls than offer guidance in how to channel that energy into the right direction, simply because they did not know what to do with those who did not conform.

A few nights after the assembly, unable to sleep, I turned on my laptop and started writing about it. For a few hours, I vented all of my feelings about all the mistakes made in schools tackling feminism, and all the wrongs that could have easily been righted. I wrote about women in the workplace, their hostility towards each other, and towards any woman who looks, thinks and feels differently, and then, in a moment of madness, I put it up on the internet for the world to see. Feeling quite proud of myself in my half-delirious state, I got back into bed, and drifted into sleep, blissfully unaware of the consequences that I was going to face the following morning.

★   ★   ★

It wasn't my smartest move, I admit. Apparently, as I was peacefully dreaming of delivering my Nobel Prize speech, overnight complaint emails from teachers had been piling up in the headteacher's inbox. I had barely stepped foot into the school building the next day when I was pulled into Mr Thorne's office. I am not saying I was expecting a promotion, but I secretly was hoping that this was an invitation to congratulate me for writing a stellar article that raised some very interesting points that he would take into consideration in future. Needless to say, what I received was a quietly terrifying Brummie bollocking, which wouldn't have looked out of place in *Peaky Blinders*.

I sat opposite Mr Thorne, feeling tiny in the large chair I was sitting in. He took a few moments finishing off typing something on his computer, before turning to me. I wondered if I was supposed to speak first and was thinking of what to say when he finally spoke.

'Yes, Mayrine.' He rubbed his hands together as he always did when he was about to say something serious and choosing his words carefully. 'The blog post . . .' He started slow – and the brevity of his words and the intermittent pauses were killing me. I would much rather he just shouted at me and got it over and done with. 'You do realise the severity of what you have done?'

I had never heard Mr Thorne sound so stern before. My hands were so tightly clasped together that I had left nail marks on my skin.

He continued, 'You raise some serious allegations, and many of them can be construed as workplace bullying.' He paused again.

'I didn't mean . . .' I began.

'If this was the case, Mayrine, I would have hoped you would have come to tell me. As you can appreciate, I cannot tolerate this in my school.'

What may have seemed like a good idea in the middle of the night had turned into my worst nightmare. In no way had I considered the repercussions of my actions.

'Sir, I just . . .' I tried to explain, but he didn't let me finish.

'I need you to be really open and frank with me, so I know exactly what's been going on.' His tone was firm. 'And then I can conduct a formal investigation.'

At the sound of those words, I wished the ground would swallow me. I had managed to outdo my own Action Plan and upgrade myself to the last step before losing my job. I knew there was no point in trying to defend myself – I would only sound like a bumbling fool. (At the time, I didn't know it was a prerequisite to become a prime minister.) Instead, I sat there, with an enlarged pink nose, at the brink of tears and looking like a traumatised Rudolph. At the pitiful sight of me, Mr Thorne softened.

'I didn't mean to cause trouble,' and the tears poured out.

'I know you would never be malicious, Mayrine,' he said, 'but I'd like to know what made you take this step.'

Honesty is the best policy, I thought. I started from the beginning, explaining about the response to *The Taming of the Shrew*, the assembly, and the students' reaction to it. Instead of being angry at me, Mr Thorne seemed genuinely upset that I felt the school wasn't doing enough to engage the female students. He asked for any suggestions I had about improving their involvement. As I desperately searched for ways to wriggle my way out of the incredibly sticky situation with my job still intact, I had an epiphany.

'I . . . I could run an after-school girls' group?' I offered. 'I could do it once a week, working with girls across the year groups who we identify as needing extra support? I could book a classroom, I could speak to the Heads of Years and create a target list of students by the end of the day?'

The offer of an additional voluntary intervention completely diverted his attention from my blog and we began to create a schedule. He asked for a written document outlining the short-term plan, and I nodded like a Churchill dog. To my utter amazement, the meeting ended on a miraculous high for both parties.

As I thanked him and walked towards the door, Mr Thorne called after me and added, 'And Mayrine . . . it's probably best you delete that blog post, eh?' with what I am convinced was a conspiratorial wink.

The group initially consisted of eight girls from Years 9 and 10 who were academically underachieving, but we also included girls we perceived as vulnerable. Over time, we ended up with eighteen girls on the register across all year groups, and a free pass for other girls to join the second half. For an hour and a half after school, every week, we sat down and talked about what it meant to be a woman. My colleagues dropped in every now and then, before they made their way home, and joined the chat; it added something to hear a variety of voices – and it made the students speak up more too. We didn't always have serious, in-depth discussions and debates at our meetings – that's not what the girls' group was about. Sometimes, I listened to them sharing stories: they were growing up; their bodies were changing, and it meant they had somewhere to go to where they could safely ask questions about things like acne or sex or feminine hygiene.

For so many of these girls, there wasn't someone at home who could teach them how to shower properly, or advise them what products to use when cleaning themselves, or explain how to deal with period pains. Considering how many hours we spent at school, it was hardly surprising that many girls started their first period at school with us, rather than at home. They thought it was hilarious when I told them that I started mine during a French test and had to try and tell my teacher in French, as English was banned in that class.

I didn't have all the answers and I didn't pretend to – sometimes we researched together. The first time one of my students tested positive with gonorrhoea, I was as clueless as her about how to deal with it, but we worked through it together with the help of Google and the school nurse. But some things I did know about: I was all-too familiar with the feeling of getting bullied for having a monobrow; I knew what it felt like to have your body shape scrutinised according to changing trends, and I was learning about the emerging pressure of social media along with the students. There were a lot of the things I wish I knew as a young girl, and I wanted these children to be able to ask any questions without fear of judgement, rather than pretending these issues don't exist or belittling them. The PSHE curriculum in schools is often just a tick-box exercise that teachers resent, or are not fully trained to deliver. Of course there are always important boundaries in teachers revealing their own personal lives to their students, but what these girls needed was someone they looked up to to reassure them that what they were thinking and feeling was normal. To know that I had been there too.

Over the course of these sessions, I heard and saw some truly shocking things, and it was clear that the sexual landscape in particular had shifted a long way from my schooldays. Listening to the girls, I learned they were having sex much earlier, with more people, and doing things that I hadn't even heard of when I was thirteen. They had to navigate their own desires alongside male desire, all in the context of a perilous online world. Sometimes I could get my head around the new era, other times I was shocked, and on one occasion I was really upset. It was when a twelve-year-old girl, Isabella, told me she had got into trouble because she had been giving head in the boys' toilet in exchange for Skittles.

Yes, you read that correctly. This twelve-year-old child was performing blow jobs in the toilets to boys in exchange for sweets. The issue came to light when a teacher noticed an unusually long queue outside the boys' toilets for a few days and eventually found out what had been going on. Meanwhile boys were going around the school corridors talking about the girl who wanted to 'taste the rainbow', because to them it was a joke. Nothing more. The girl's mother was called into school, and they sat down with the Head of Year. What was most upsetting is that Isabella seemed genuinely unfazed, unable to see why people had made such a big deal about this and why she couldn't continue. She wanted Skittles, she explained earnestly, and this way she could have lots of them.

There are so many questions that come to mind when you find yourself in the midst of such an unprecedented situation: why did these boys think it was okay to use a young girl in this way? How on earth does a twelve-year-old child even think to do such a thing? Who first came up with the idea? How could the adults around her not have noticed how she saw herself? Unfortunately, there isn't one solid answer, because there are so many different factors at play. And we start with the hyper-sexualisation of women in the media.

When young people are idolising pop stars and singing along to lyrics that claim a woman's power is obtained from the size of her arse or her ability to perform oral sex, it could be argued that they become immune to the true meaning and consequences of the words. For so many of these girls – particularly for those who aren't incredibly academically high-achieving – they feel a better life, money, fame and any sense of worth can only be obtained as a result of Instagram fame, and by monetising their looks and bodies. And of course, there is an endless line of men and boys who encourage that view. Around the same time that 'the Isabella incident' was being investigated, one of the most famous British 'influencers' was a teenage girl from London herself, who many of our students followed. I'm not going to disclose her 'stage name' for obvious reasons, but she gained fame and notoriety by performing oral sex on a social-media platform, and her business grew at such an exponential rate that after a few months, she announced a UK tour. She had expanded her team to include five new girls to join her venture and there were posters all over social media as if this was a Little Mix concert, with a list of dates and cities that they would be visiting. She herself was a product of a society where a woman's sexual self is often presented as her only form of power, and this was the kind of representation my girls had access to. And though I am sure there were plenty of other women who could be held as examples of success, how many of them were relatable and realistically achievable? If you don't look like Mary Berry, or don't speak like Fiona Bruce, how can you aspire to be them?

Though we did everything we could to keep the situation within a small group, it was inevitable that news of Isabella's circumstance would spread through the school. Her Head of Year tried to organise a counsellor, but due to budget cuts, it took a while to get the appointment. We eventually managed, and I hope that she reached some understanding of what happened and never felt like she was to blame. I didn't teach Isabella, so I wasn't involved in the details of what happened afterwards, but I was part of many conversations in the girls' group about it. We spoke about consent, about the value of sexual acts, the expectations of boys. Many of the girls were distressed by the story, but sadly many of them weren't that surprised. It was a terrible story, but it opened a door into even more honesty in our discussions. One thing that came up time and time again in our honest conversations about sex was the role of mobile phones and social media.

Fortunately, my school years preceded smartphones; my first phone was a Nokia 8210 and the most exciting function on that was 'Snake'. But these kids were growing up online, so their personal lives were their public lives, and this blurring was damaging. I saw the presence of nudes rapidly escalate during my time in teaching and it became something I dealt with regularly – at least once a week. Girls were sending photos either in their underwear or fully nude, nearly always to a boy they thought they loved. The boys often didn't want to 'make it official', so sending provocative pictures was a way the girls thought they could impress them. Of course, the images would never remain private by their intended recipient and soon they would be all around the school – and often around other local schools. It was a vicious cycle of insecurity leading to social media, and social media leading to more insecurities.

Ceylan was one of those girls. After the topless image that she had sent in confidence was passed around the whole school, her father was informed and called into a meeting to discuss the matter further. Because I had known Ceylan for so long, I knew about how much her family was struggling since her mother's death, and I also knew there was a good chance this could be the final straw for their relationship, which was already hanging by a thread. But as her sole guardian we had very little choice but to call in her father and have a meeting with Ceylan present. I wished he could have been there more for her after her mother's passing, that he could have shown her love and that she was valued. And I wish I didn't have to show them both the image.

He didn't take the phone from me. He took one glimpse of the image, looked away again, from the phone, from us, from his daughter. He was still, but you could see his pulse beating in his neck. The room was silent, and the silence was deafening. I cannot describe the heartbreak on both their faces. Ceylan was a neglected child who had faced immense tragedy and was craving acceptance, and her father was a broken man who had never, ever envisaged such a moment in his life and didn't have a wife to help him deal with it. As Mr Fieldhouse went through the legal implications of such private and intimate images being shared in the public domain, neither of them said a word, and when the meeting came to a close, Ceylan's father silently walked out of the room alone, leaving her seated alone in front of us. The second she heard the door shut, she burst into inconsolable tears, not just at the thought of losing her privacy, but also at the thought of losing her one remaining parent.

We often talk about the impact of absent – or distant – fathers on sons, but we don't discuss the impact a missing or a flawed male role model has on daughters, aside from the occasional snide accusation of someone having 'daddy issues'. I saw numerous cases of girls like Ceylan who desperately craved love and affection from a male figure, and if they didn't receive that, they went searching for that happiness elsewhere, usually in places that were not worthy of them or good for them. They threw themselves into compromising situations, all in a quest to feel valued, wanted and protected.

Ceylan's father decided that it would be best if she moved out of our school – a decision I understood but didn't agree with. The boy who was really at fault here endured not a single repercussion, and yet Ceylan was punished and vilified, because society blames women for men's actions and excuses their wrongdoings. But there was very little we could do. We could only hope that Ceylan's father didn't shut the door on her forever and that she didn't let that one naïve decision define the rest of her life.

The more I spoke to the girls in my group, or my class, or just in the corridor, the more I was able to figure feminism out for myself. In a department of twenty-five strong-willed, independent, capable, opinionated women, we weren't always going to get along, and sometimes it felt like that's what the patriarchy wanted from us. It didn't matter if we didn't always agree, or see eye-to-eye; we learned to see each other as friends. The endless sharing of resources, cups of tea, gossip, banter, advice and consolation became our strength in dealing with the daily obstacles.

When women support each other, it can be the most powerful force ever. Where would I be without Aurea's friendship and Ms Lewis's guidance? I would have survived, yes, but it would have been a whole lot harder and a lot less fun. And though it took time for me to find my place in it, we were a team – and all of us knew that we could go to each other at any time, with any concern, and we would be supported. We celebrated births together and held each other during bereavements. We covered for each other when we were sick and guarded the office door when we needed privacy. I organised Aurea's hen-party, and got into massive trouble – again – when my email got flagged because of the rude words in it (a whole other story for a whole other day). I sat with Holly – the one who completed my love triangle with Aurea – and planned our spa breaks for the half-term. I cried until my eyes were swollen and laughed until my belly ached, in what was the best, most random, most eclectic, most formidable friendship group you could ever imagine. We were different in so many ways but we found a common ground of rooting for each other.

The journey developed in a similar way in my girls' group. At first, bringing together a group of strong personalities, who were too different – or even too similar – meant that clashes were inevitable. But the fact that we had girls of different backgrounds meant that once they did form a bond, it could only be described as an awakening. Over time, as they worked together, opened up to one another, I watched them learn to understand and to empathise with each other. I saw the amazing thing a friendship in girls can be as they morphed into a support system. And that friendship was so important for girls who were struggling with so much confusion.

Feminism is only really possible when women champion each other, whatever their differences. As Audre Lorde said, 'I am not free while any woman is unfree, even when her shackles are very different from my own.'

There isn't a 'one size fits all' feminism and it's only when we come together as women that we can help the girls under our care.

6

Boys Need Guidance from Many Places

If you look at the maneater I am today, you would never have suspected I had almost no interaction with boys growing up. My own brother was twelve years older than me so I couldn't use him as a case study, I wasn't allowed to talk to boys until I was at university and I went to a girls' school, so the inner workings of the minds of teenage boys remained a mystery to me until I became a teacher.

Being thrown straight into the deep end, almost as soon as I enlisted, was a fascinating learning curve. On one particular lunchtime, three years into my job, I was sitting in my classroom systematically rejecting and blocking students' friend requests on Facebook, when Martin, a boy in Year 10, came in looking distraught. I remember Martin extremely fondly because he often said what most boys were thinking but would never dare say for fear of being mocked or punished. Martin had no such filter and I found his grown-up musings about the world insightful and hugely endearing. He sometimes stuck his head round the door as he walked past my classroom and shouted 'HEY, MISS BAIGEL!', but as I looked up that day, I could sense that this was a little more than a casual visit.

'Are you OK, darling?'

Not good. That one question opened a whole can of worms and before I could say another word, Martin – a six-foot-one, hefty boy – was lying on my classroom floor, bawling his eyes out. There he lay, tears streaming down his face, and panic swept over me like a wave. I had no idea what to do about it.

'What's happened, Martin?' asked, trying to remain calm. Simultaneously, I kept glancing at the door, praying that Aurea or Holly, or anyone, would come to look for me.

'NO ONE WILL HAVE SEX WITH ME,' Martin blurted out. 'I WILL NEVER GET TO SHAG GIRLS LIKE THE OTHER BOYS.'

I took a deep breath. I felt ill-equipped on two fronts, communicating with a child who was so emotionally distraught and trying to give sex advice. My mum didn't even like it if I said the word 'sex', let alone talked about the act, and counselling a young man about his needs and desires, an area I was certainly no expert in myself, was daunting to say the least.

'Of course it will happen for you,' I said, trying not to sound awkward, but sounding deeply, deeply awkward. 'It may happen later, like at college.'

'BUT WHAT IF IT DOESN'T?' he continued, head in his hands. 'What if you are lying too . . . just like the rest of them?' His voice had quietened, as if he were deep in reflection. 'Sometimes,' he added after a pause. 'Sometimes, I think of killing myself, but I can't, because THEN I'LL DIE A VIRGIN AND NOT EVEN KNOW WHAT IT IS LIKE.' He opened his eyes for a moment to see my face and my heart broke for him. How was I supposed to know what to say?

'Martin, when it does happen for you, it will be special,' I improvised, cringing myself out. 'But you can't force these things. You need to just wait it out and it will happen naturally.'

'IT WON'T. IT WON'T. THE OTHER BOYS DON'T HAVE TO WAIT. THEY GET ANY GIRL THEY WANT. I DON'T WANT TO BE A VIRGIN ANY MORE SO THEN I CAN DIE IN PEACE!'

I was stunned and drained and wanted to cry and laugh and hug him and run. Luckily for me, Aurea had finally heard the screaming and came in, gently pacifying Martin out of my room. She turned to face me at the door and, with a cheeky wink, only said, 'Sex therapist now, Baigel?'

The story spread around the school like wildfire, over-heard by children in the corridor and passed on as a big joke. I planned to keep a low profile until my reputation as the students' sex guru became yesterday's news. So, I was lurking in my classroom a couple of days later when I had a surprise visitor: Mr Wilson, holding a slightly greasy box, and ner-vously standing at my door. My heart skipped a beat, quite literally, and I willed myself to stay cool.

'Are they for me?' I said flirtatiously, gesturing towards the chicken wings.

'Yeah,' he grinned warmly, coming further into the room. 'You didn't come down for lunch today. I thought you might be hungry.'

'I'm always hungry,' I said, but then immediately worried that it may have come across like an innuendo. 'I get hangry when I'm hungry,' I added. I would kill myself later. 'That's so thoughtful of you! Thank you!'

He paused awkwardly, then replied, 'No problem,' and handed me the box.

He stood watching me for a moment as I started eating it straight away with my hands in true Pakistani style, but remembering he was watching, I tried to transform my uncouth actions into a more delicate and graceful manoeuvre.

He raised his hand and said, 'Just let me know if you want anything else.' Before I had the opportunity to respond with 'Just you', he had turned to leave the room.

As he walked towards the door again, I added, 'It's finger-lickin' good.' Confused, he nodded and left, and I flopped back in my chair, absolutely mortified.

Those two instances were filled with more testosterone than I could handle. Yet I had no choice but to work out what sort of support the boys needed and just . . . grow a pair. A certain Hot Maths Teacher was one matter, and I had no idea what to do about that without literally throwing myself in his path like a Japanese Nyotaimori. However, I knew I had to apply myself to figure out my male students. Understanding their needs, thoughts and struggles would be valuable going forward. For all the jokes and memes about the simplicity of boys and complexity of girls, actually understanding the sensitivity required when communicating effectively with boys was nothing less than a craft. Getting through to them without 'exposing' them as weak in front of their peers, offering support without insinuating they're not 'masculine' enough to cope by themselves, disciplining them without triggering a violent reaction, all required expertise. Martin's outburst was just a verbalisation of one example of the pressure facing boys, but the challenges facing boys were so widespread, and their experience was so far removed from my own, that for a long time it was difficult to know how to help them.

★　　★　　★

The majority of my male students were much taller and stronger than me, but they still looked to me for protection. All five foot two of me. Letting them down wasn't an option, even if it meant risking my life – and on one occasion, I had to put my money where my mouth was. I had finished for the day, and after blowing Ms Lewis a kiss through her office window, I wearily trudged towards the school gate and started to make my way home. My feet were aching and I pulled out my phone to ask my mum what she had cooked. As I reached the high road, I saw that Mr Wilson was the teacher assigned to patrolling after school and I waved excitedly. He grinned and came over to me and we stood there, talking for a bit. The conversation flowed so naturally that even when I said goodbye, he continued walking with me towards the station, chatting away.

But as we got nearer to my destination, he suddenly seemed distracted. I followed his gaze and noticed a small group that had formed across the road; it seemed as though some unfamiliar boys had approached one of our Year 11 students. They weren't in school uniform, though they looked quite young, and at first, it was difficult to tell what they were all discussing. Before I could even process what was happening, Mr Wilson had started to run towards them, shouting for them to stop. Within seconds, our student, Shaun, was on the floor, repeatedly being kicked in the head by the group of boys around him.

I instinctively ran towards the scene. I genuinely don't even know what help I thought I could possibly offer in the situation, but instinct overcomes rationality sometimes. Your own emotions and welfare take a back seat because your priority is to emotionally and physically safeguard the children under your care. In the melee, I saw the glint of a blade and hoped it was only going to be used as a threat – but I don't doubt that if any one of us had said the wrong word at that point, it would have been used. If I'm completely honest, it's all a blur now, but at the sight of 'teachers', particularly Mr Wilson, the attackers got onto their bikes and rode off. We were lucky – kids don't care about size and age anymore because they no longer fight with their hands.

We carried Shaun back to school, bleeding from his mouth, barely able to stand from the head injuries he had sustained.

'That's the second time they've got me,' he mumbled in a daze. 'I need to get to my grandpa's eightieth birthday party.'

I knew Shaun – a bright, well-behaved student who never got into any trouble or fights at school. He wasn't just roaming the streets. He wasn't a member of any gang. Yet he told me that these boys – school age themselves – were riding around the high road after school and targeted him because they recognised that he wasn't from their postcode and wanted to claim their territory. What would have happened if we hadn't intervened at that particular moment? Shaun's family would have received a phone call saying their son had been stabbed – or worse. And the media coverage would have insinuated that he deserved it.

We drove Shaun home, in a sad, stunned silence. I sat next to him in the back so I could keep an eye on how he was feeling. He rested his head on the window, looking out of the glass, his mouth hanging slightly open from where his lip was so swollen. In front of him, Mr Wilson had his eyes fixed firmly on the road, with a slight frown noticeable on his forehead. I wanted to talk to Shaun about what had just happened, but I didn't know what to say. As we got closer to his house, the best I could come out with was, 'Are you

OK?' For a moment, I thought neither of them had heard what I had said, because there wasn't even a flicker of recognition, but then, still looking out of the window, Shaun spoke.

'It's been a bad year for me,' he said. I wasn't even sure if he was speaking to me or just thinking aloud. 'There isn't long left until my GCSEs and I don't think I'm going to get the grades I need for college. I don't want to stay around here.'

'What subject are you most worried about?' I asked.

'Maths,' he said. 'English I'm OK with. I have Ms Bloome. She's good.'

'I can help you with Maths, Shaun,' Mr Wilson finally spoke. 'If you need extra help, we can revise together in my room, whenever you're free.' Shaun didn't reply.

'I just want to make my mum proud,' he whispered. We drove the rest of the way in silence.

My heart ached. If that was any other person – a girl, an adult, a middle-class child growing up in a middle-class area – they would probably receive months of therapy after such an ordeal. They would need counselling. They would be traumatised, unable to walk those same streets for many months, or even years. But this boy, because he was a teenage Black boy living in Tottenham, couldn't say he was scared. He had to go to school the next day and travel home via that same high road, where he could potentially run into the same boys for a third time. This fifteen-year-old boy had to put on a brave face and not talk about the trauma, his feelings or emotions, because he had to accept that this was just a regular part of life. A life where he was nearly killed for no apparent reason, on his way to his granddad's birthday after school.

So what would happen if Shaun started carrying a knife too, just to feel safe the next time he ran into the same boys or a similar situation? Would we call him a criminal? One option in the past would have been to ask our resident school police officer to patrol the high road after school every day, whose job it was to intervene if any student was suspected of committing or at the risk of being victim of any criminal activity. He was also often used to give 'talks' to children who needed some legal guidance if needed.

But with the Tory cuts, specifically the removal of 21,000 police officers, we now had to share our police officer with two other schools. That meant teachers were asked to take turns monitoring the streets after school on the days he wasn't with us, supervising the bus stops and ensuring our kids got home safely. When we trained to teach Maths and English, not once did we think that we would be putting our own lives at risk as part of the job – without any extra bonus or incentive for doing so.

And even if we informed the local police station, let's be honest, they were just as stretched as we were; if not more. They didn't have the funding and resources available to deal with all the knife-crime cases and young muggings and violence – unless and until someone died. But say they did manage to find out who the perpetrators were, the most they would do is possibly visit their house and warn them. And what would be the impact of their visit? The next day, the same boys would be roaming the streets again – but this time, the consequences would be worse because this time, they would know that the victim 'snitched'. That is why these kids don't speak. That is why no one speaks.

My years of teaching were full of amazing success stories. Boys like Yakub, who went on to set up a charity that provided medical aid for a number of villages in Kenya, and Lewis, whose directorial debut was screened at The BFI London Film Festival. There are so many boys I remember for their triumphs, though sadly, it's the stories of boys who were let down by the system that I recall most vividly. What happened to Shaun was just a tiny glimpse of the violence which infiltrated the world my boys were trying to navigate.

I taught students who were walking home from volunteering at youth centres when a car pulled up next to them and shots were fired through the window, leaving them bleeding to death with bullets in their chest. I taught students who were caught in the crossfire of a 'postcode war', where N22 didn't like N15, so gangs would attack rivals if they stepped foot in the wrong street. Boys as young as ten were witnessing stabbings, shootings and death at such close proximity that often they learned to normalise it and sometimes became susceptible to it, purely for their own protection. You don't need a degree in psychotherapy to know what it would do to a child to see his best friend or brother get murdered in front of his eyes.

What struck me most, watching it happen so closely to students I loved, and watching it happen so often, was the gradual decline in the value of human life. These students who live a life of poverty and hardship and challenge, almost became immune to death the more they were exposed to it – it was inevitable. As an outsider, I could see all the life they still had to live, and everything they still had to look forward to, but they didn't feel like they had anything to lose.

Less than two weeks before the GCSEs, Marvin was

absent from his English lesson. It was a lower set and a small class, so we pushed all the tables together, sat in a circle and worked through texts and exam questions as a group, and Marvin's spot was always next to me. I thought he might turn up late so we left his seat empty, but he didn't, and I wondered where he was. Regardless of how Marvin behaved in other lessons, it wasn't like him to miss English – and especially not this close to the exams.

As the lesson finished and the students began to pack away, I asked them to pass a message on for me.

'If you see Marvin,' I said, 'let him know I'm not happy with him . . . and show him the notes from today's lesson, please.'

They laughed at my pitiful attempt to be stern, whilst I collected Marvin's blank practice paper and added it to my already overspilling desk. Just then, there was a gentle knock at the door. Mr Abara was standing in the doorway with a slightly concealed figure skulking behind him.

'Ms Baig,' he said, 'I have a young man here who would like to say something to you.'

I moved closer to where they were standing and saw Marvin, with his jacket on and hood up, looking down at his feet. My immediate thought was that he had been caught truanting and I felt hurt that he wanted to miss my lesson.

'Where were you today, Marvin?' I asked. Mr Abara looked at Marvin, waiting for him to speak.

'Take your hood off, please,' Mr Abara said, and quietly, Marvin took his hood off and looked up. His entire right eye was swollen in a giant purplish bruise.

'What happened?' I asked. Marvin didn't speak.

'Marvin got himself into some trouble yesterday night, Miss,' Mr Abara explained, in his usual collected manner, 'and he was too embarrassed to face you, so he came to me for his English lesson. He said he didn't want to disappoint you.' Marvin still didn't meet my eye.

'Can I leave him with you, Miss?' Mr Abara said.

'Yes,' I replied. 'Marvin, can you come inside, please?' As I heard him settling into a seat, I thanked Mr Abara for bringing Marvin to me.

'That's OK, Miss. It's amazing, isn't it? He gets into grown-up trouble out of school, but, put him in front of you and he's a child again.'

I nodded, considering what he had just said, and turned around to re-enter my classroom. I sat next to Marvin, and we both didn't look at each other. He was staring at the table and I was wondering where to even begin. In a couple of weeks, I knew I wouldn't see him again, and so every word I said mattered. I spoke carefully, weightily.

'I need you to understand . . . the trouble you're going to get yourself into if you carry on getting involved in this . . . stuff . . . outside of school,' I said. He listened. 'You have an opportunity, Marvin . . . to get some decent GCSEs, go to college, and live a good, peaceful life. If you keep getting involved in bad things outside of schoo . . .'

'It doesn't matter, Miss,' he said. I waited to see if he would elaborate, but he didn't.

'What doesn't matter?' I challenged – but he stayed quiet.

I looked at him, his head bowed, his body language defeated and I felt myself losing my temper. It didn't happen often. Most of the time, it was just for show. But I couldn't have pretended, even if I tried.

'It doesn't matter if you end up dead or in prison? It doesn't matter to who, Marvin? It doesn't matter to you? Because it does matter to your mum, it does matter to your friends who were all asking where you were today, and it bloody matters to me, because if it didn't, I wouldn't be sitting here every day investing all my time and energy into you.' My voice cracked and I knew I was about to cry. Marvin was shocked and so was I. He had never seen anything but a smile on my face before and he didn't know how to react to my words. I tried to compose myself. 'You can do something with your life, Marvin,' I said gently. 'I want you to have a good life. You deserve to have a good life.'

The first time I heard about a child getting involved with gang activities, it was so shocking. Gang affiliations weren't common in our school – in fact, they were almost unheard of at first. I joined the school immediately after the London riots, and my headteacher prided himself on having zero students associated with them. As the years went by, whispers began to surface – but still not a lot. But by the time I was twenty-six, we were having meetings every week about gang culture because it had become endemic in local schools. Along with cuts to schools, libraries, mental-health services and social care, the government shut down youth centres, resulting in nowhere for young people to go. Without parents organising gymnastics classes and ballet lessons to fill up the evenings, these kids were left with nothing to do in their spare time, leaving them unprotected on lawless streets. With a lack of suitable male role models and often absent fathers, I saw the longing for a figure to look up to in so many of my students, drawing them towards a dark world they were far too young to fully understand the dangers of.

For so many children, the streets provided a sense of protection, belonging and purpose and – what they perceived to be – loyalty, from their gang members. They finally found someone to teach them how to talk to girls, make money, work out, play football – all the things that they weren't being offered elsewhere. Their vulnerabilities were exploited by the older members for their own gain. It was a form of grooming, often starting off with as little as giving the 'youngers' £50 here and there to carry out little tasks for them, some money to buy new trainers or a nice meal, but it would serve to ingratiate them amongst the ranks of the gangs and they wouldn't ever want to leave. In a choice between belonging and loneliness, it wasn't a hard decision for some.

You would be surprised at how many boys were lured into bad choices due to the financial strain of supporting a family, rather than vainglory or street credibility. After I finally got off the naughty step I was permanently on in the first few years of my career, I was selected to go to an 'Outstanding teacher training', and part of that course meant I visited other schools around London to observe and hone good practice. I'd spend a few days a month in another school, observing lessons of experienced teachers who were considered 'lead practitioners', speaking to the students and learning from the staff. Every week, I attended a pastoral meeting with Heads of Years and Heads of Departments where students who were identified as causes for concern were discussed, and intervention measures were put in place. In one of these schools, I met a young man called Fahim who, at face value, was the popular football player, who always had lots of female attention and male friends.

He seemed to pop up everywhere, always at the centre of conversations or being put forward by teachers to be the face of the school. On one afternoon, I was sitting in a Year 9 History lesson, and the students were sharing their paragraphs on the causes behind World War I, when Fahim turned up at the door to give a notice to the teacher. One boy with a cowlick and pimples was in the middle of reading his work out, so Fahim waited at the door. The boy was reading slowly, using his finger to follow the words and got to the part where 'Rio Ferdinand came and got shot.'

'Oh my days!' a boy with a distinct Irish accent shouted out. 'You're so dumb!' Others followed suit, shouting out insults and mimicking the boy, who was pink with shame. Fahim, who had been watching everything from the door, coolly walked in and handed the letter to the teacher.

As he turned to leave, he looked at the class, and with his usual cheeky grin said, 'I used to get confused between Franz and Rio all the time. It's mad. I thought it was just me.' The students who were laughing quietened down to hear Fahim speak, and the cowlick kid looked dumbfounded that Fahim was even talking to him.

'Yeah, that's true, you know,' the Irish boy piped up. 'You have to remember so many names in History! I used to think Anne Boleyn was one of Henry VIII's wives.'

'Erm . . . she was,' Fahim laughed, and as he left the class-room, a chorus of kids had found a new target, and Cowlick's cool ratings had severely increased.

I looked forward to seeing Fahim when I went to his school, until in one weekly 'student concerns' meeting, we were told that Fahim's house had been raided by the police at 5 a.m. that morning and he had been arrested. As the teachers discussed the next steps for the school, I sat there in shock. It just hadn't crossed my mind that he was the sort of kid to get into that kind of trouble. But I immediately felt angry with myself because I'd fallen into the trap of thinking there was 'that sort of kid'. The truth is, it could happen to anyone.

I learned that at home, Fahim was the only son of an elderly father, and his mother was a housewife who spoke very little English. Fahim was responsible for putting food on the table each day and managing the day-to-day running of the household. He'd done that since he was barely in double digits. He had four younger sisters, who all needed to get married one day, and as the eldest son of a Bangladeshi family, it was his responsibility to ensure that his whole family's complex needs were met. So what does such a boy do? When the opportunity arose to earn some much-needed cash, of course he took it. In return for selling substances, he was able to ensure stability for his family. And his family, so desperate for the support, did not question how and why a child of a young age had access to that much money, as long as he was providing for his family and ensuring the bills were paid for. They turned a blind eye to their single source of provision because of their poverty.

The demonisation of boys like Fahim is easy to do from an outside perspective, but when Fahim's struggle – the pressure and the responsibility – is laid bare in front of you, it isn't quite so easy to be so disparaging. There is a strong distinction between criminality and hardship, and although Dickens repeatedly wrote about it nearly two centuries ago, trying to make society see this, it seems like the message is still falling on deaf ears.

The teacher training taught me a lot. Yes, it taught me about other practices and techniques, but more than that it taught me that each and every school had an issue with boys being left behind and getting into trouble.

One of the greatest successes of our school was the fact that all the staff mirrored the students in terms of racial diversity, background and cultural heritage. This was a very deliberate decision made by Mr Thorne when he recruited new teachers – he ensured that he kept the ethnic make-up of the kids at heart, so the students had people to look up to in order to know that success was possible. It meant that these students often had role models standing in front of them who understood their lives, their backgrounds – they had faced the same challenges, they were into similar things, they understood cultural nuances but had made different choices. And because they had been in similar positions themselves, they were willing to go above and beyond to ensure the students reached their potential, and offered them alternative options to turn their lives around.

Yasser was an example of a boy who turned his life around, due to his incredible hard work and focus which was supported by dedicated teachers. I first met him when he was fourteen: I remember him misspelling 'lose' as 'loose', and then telling me 'But Miss, "losing" isn't in my vocabulary.' Yasser did everything in a fast pace, as if he was rushing to finish. He entered the room in haste, completed his work at superhuman speed and his temper erupted with a similar rashness. He was a complete contrast to his older sister, who was incredibly calm and conscientious, and was Head Girl of our school at the time. It was Mr Clarke, the PE teacher's idea to channel Yasser's energy into some sort of physical activity, and they began by entering him into an inter-school 100-metre competition. He won – and three months down the line, he had won the regional tournament too and been crowned the fastest runner in Haringey.

Mr Clarke spoke to Yasser's parents about the possibility of signing Yasser up to a running club with a professional coach. His parents had moved to the UK, like many, with a dream of making a better life for themselves and their children and were passionate about their children's education and progression, but they explained that with their working hours and the other siblings to take care of, there would be no one to take Yasser to the training sessions. That could have easily been the end of Yasser's competitive career. But Mr Clarke refused to accept the loss of an opportunity that had Yasser's name written all over it. When Mr Clarke was a young boy, he was scouted by Brentford, but his mum was unable to take him to his trials. Though he seemed quite content with his stardom in the school grounds, he was willing to go the extra mile – literally – to ensure another boy didn't fall by the wayside. So, he organised to take Yasser to training for the rest of the year, driving for hours several times a week. When Yasser returned after the summer holidays in Year 10, he was a new boy with a new focus. By Year 11, he was training to represent England.

Then there was Marvin who, in the summer, two years after his brother's exclusion, opened his GCSE envelope, only to discover that he had passed English and had done enough to get on to his college course. Who would have ever thought that Marvin would be the one celebrating this achievement? He raced around the hall showing everyone who was there his unexpected result. We stood, all in tears, and I tried to call his mum to share the news with her, but she didn't pick up. My mind wandered to James and I hoped he was able to see similar success somewhere else in a couple of years too.

These successes didn't happen by chance. Yasser's immense talent could very easily have gone unnoticed or disappeared into oblivion had the school not chosen to prioritise it, and Marvin could have easily become just another statistic. But the headteacher, and the hundreds of staff members, worked tirelessly every day to improve the children's prospects and transformed ours into one of the few rare schools that catered to the very unique needs and demands of the community that it was a part of, constantly trying to override the damaging stereotypes about themselves and the world around them that my students were constantly exposed to.

The media propagates negative stereotypes of Black boys, Muslim boys, working-class boys, and it is difficult to imagine what it can do to a child's psyche when you are constantly bombarded with a vilified image of yourself. The children are both a product of this unhealthy social conditioning but also blamed for perpetuating it. This culture of toxic masculinity suppresses any show of emotion and stigmatises vulnerability, sometimes manifesting in the classroom as anger or aggression. The way to avoid and manage such confrontations required sensitivity, patience and tolerance, and if that didn't happen, things could go very wrong.

Mr Lever was a prime example of things going very wrong. In one of his lessons, he was shouting at his class as usual when he caught his student, Caleb, smiling. Because Mr Lever was in a particularly foul mood that day, he took this very personally and as Caleb tried to explain that he wasn't laughing at him, the debate got extremely heated. Mr Lever refused to hear any 'excuses' and told Caleb to leave the room, but he refused to budge, taking Mr Lever's attitude as a personal disrespect. This conflict, which began as the teacher's misunderstanding, rapidly escalated. As both were determined not to yield, Mr Lever decided to escort Caleb to his punishment himself, by dragging him out of the room by his jumper, in front of all the other students who were watching, horrified. By now, Mr Lever had worked himself into a state of fury whilst shame and humiliation overcame Caleb. He pulled himself back from Mr Lever and punched him in the face.

In Mr Thorne's office later that day, Mr Lever told him, 'I am taking some time off. But when I'm back, I want him gone.' And Caleb did go – but when I think about his story, all I can wonder is how dragging a boy was acceptable behaviour, particularly from a grown adult. Only one person in the story wasn't a child and he was the one who should have been able to keep his own ego and emotions in check.

Personally, since our first encounter in the staffroom after James's exclusion, I had taken a very quick dislike to Mr Lever. He had the same effect on me as a Dementor from *Harry Potter*, i.e. he sucked my soul, but he himself was a product of that same vicious cycle. I know every teacher is different, and some are strict and wonderful, and some are warm and nurturing, but my problem with him was that instead of loving the kids, and having their best interests at heart, he seemed to be in direct competition with them. The type who took great pleasure in punishing a child simply because he could. Mr Lever was a prime example of an angry young boy who grew into an angry young man. He had deep-rooted, unresolved issues and now used school as an opportunity to prove his masculinity by asserting his power over weaker boys. In the spirit of the words written by Frederick Douglass, 'It is easier to build strong boys, than to repair broken men', and part of my job as a teacher was to try and prevent any more students from becoming Mr Lever in the future.

Sometimes small tweaks make all the difference, and one I learned for successful behaviour management was to always give a reason behind the rule; if students know you are not taking personal offence but saying no because the thing in itself is not good for them, they almost always comply. A 'Don't swing on your chair, sweetheart, I don't want you to hurt yourself' would always elicit a better response than a 'Don't swing on your chair'. In my experience, students respected teachers for being strict and having strong discipline, but they also wanted that respect reciprocated – shouting and dictatorial approaches were hardly ever successful in fixing challenging behaviour.

Of course, what we deem to be 'challenging behaviour' looks different according to the type of school, the geographical location and the social and cultural make-up of the cohort. I'm not saying the only issues schools experience relating to teenage boys are gang-related – there are swathes and swathes of other unexpected misdemeanours and indiscretions children get up to, and some of the stories are quite surprising. My best friend who works in an independent school recently told me that she had a really shit day. Little did I know that she meant it literally. Basically, after a very stressful week, with lots of kids going off the rails for various reasons, she received an email from the site manager. A cleaner had complained that when she went to clean the boys' toilet, she discovered that someone had taken a dump in the bin. Half-bemused and half-mourning the state of the world, I asked her what she intended to do. She said she had to send an email around to all staff making them aware of the incident, but she wasn't exactly sure what was a feasible way of dealing with it. She couldn't tell the students because it would encourage a silly reaction or, even worse, plant the idea into their minds.

'What words did you use?' I asked.

I wasn't sure if she was stifling a laugh. She said, 'I wrote, "Someone has been defecating in the bin – I attach a picture. I would appreciate it if you could all be vigilant and report anything to me that may be of significance to the investigation."' For many days, I thought about who on earth would think to do that and what it could possibly achieve. I know I once watched a boy piss on some coursework, but this felt so . . . pre-meditated. It did make me feel appreciative of my school – which did come with its own challenging behaviour – but it seemed different. When students don't do their homework, or talk in class, or fight with each other, or even get involved in gangs or drugs or violence, it all comes from a very human place – and a relatable human experience. It usually stems from pain, or loss, or rage, or grief, or abuse, or neglect, or poverty, or sadness, or envy, or isolation and this knowledge makes it easier to try and implement some sort of intervention and support. If you know what is missing, you can try your best to fill those gaps in and help fix the problem. However, there is something unique about shitting in a bin, knowing that a cleaner would have to clean your shit, and getting a thrill about creating havoc for no real purpose. Maybe this story represents that there are issues in all parts of society, or maybe this was, in fact, a cry for help, but I wonder as a teacher how you would even begin to unpick and resolve such behaviour.

Of course all children, across all types of schools, have the same capacity for love and the same need for love, but it was clear to me after a few years into teaching, that our boys needed a very specific sort of care and attention.

There are significant pedagogical differences when it came to teaching boys, but that isn't because of genetic disparities – it is because of what society has done to them.

7

You Can't Beat the System (But Sometimes You Can Get Round It)

When the senior leadership team decided to launch a new reading initiative to improve literacy standards across the school, we were all asked to name our classrooms after our favourite writers. My classroom was wedged in between 'Shakespeare Shack' and 'Harper Lee Lounge', and I stood outside for a while, contemplating its literary fate. I stared at it for ages, like you stare at a newborn baby, wondering what to call it. I considered 'Chaucer Chamber', but it felt a bit sinister for a room full of children, and 'Dickens Den' didn't quite give off the right vibe. I scanned the room searching for some inspiration, and finally it came to me. I stuck a massive sign on the door saying 'Kinsella Corner', named after Sophie Kinsella, author of the *Shopaholic* series.

My room was overflowing with so much paraphernalia, the name was a perfect fit. My cupboard was full of cardigans and spare tights, and my drawers stuffed with cute, pastel-coloured highlighters and other stationery that was too pretty to use but too pretty not to buy. The secret shoe collection under my desk had significantly grown over the years, and I also kept my bottles of body mist under there, hidden from the students. The boys had recently found the spray and Omar, one of the Casanovas of the school, started a trend of spraying himself with it after the lesson. When Abdullah asked him what he was doing, he insisted, 'The gyaldem love it when you smell like them. Truss me.' And that was it. There was a queue of teenage boys fighting each other, shouting 'Spray me! Spray me!' Now, thanks to Victoria's Secret, there were a bunch of fourteen-year-old boys walking around the school, smelling like strawberries.

Scattered across the top of the desk were hundreds of cards and random items that my students had given to me as Christmas presents. Many of them couldn't afford to buy fancy things, so the majority of my gifts were homemade, like 'spicy lip balm' and 'a jar of memories'. Remembering my own homemade efforts for the teachers I'd liked, I was touched and couldn't bear to throw anything away. The thought and effort made the presents infinitely more special than an overpriced bottle of alcohol.

I didn't just choose the name because I saw myself in Becky Bloomwood. I wanted an author who felt relatable, human, or at least someone who hadn't died well over a hundred years ago. I pulled my kids through Shakespeare and Dickens, although, to some of them, they were in a different language, but there'd been other times I'd seen a Jacqueline Wilson paperback poking out of one of their bags, or watched a few of them swap *Diary of a Wimpy Kid* books with each other. These kids may have felt alienated by the old-fashioned curriculum, but I knew if I could match the right book to the kid, I could ignite a flame within them, a burning passion for literature, which even Prometheus couldn't steal.

There was never any question in my mind about teaching English. The marking was awful, the workload was crazy because every single student had at least four English lessons a week, and you had to listen to some quite staggering misinterpretations of the most beautiful books in the language. But I do feel like reading somewhat saved me. Since I was two years old, my sister would sit with me for hours upstairs, reading children's books and fairy tales. She would share stories about lavish feasts and extravagant castles, as I let the world of imagination fill in the gaps of my existence. When I was twelve, she introduced me to Judy Blume, and I learned about bras and periods and 'two minutes in the closet' for the first time in *Are You There God? It's Me, Margaret*. My mum took us to the local library and we would sit for hours, devouring a book a day. Falling in love with books changed my life, and once I decided to be a teacher, there was no doubt that I wanted to help other children find that pleasure.

There's no denying the fact a lot of our students hated English, found reading painfully boring, and couldn't have cared less about why Oliver asked for more. And for some of them, reading was just so difficult. Inner-city schools have serious problems with literacy, and I saw children struggling with reading all the time. There are lots of reasons for low literacy rates, from English not being spoken at home, to limited access to reading materials, to parents who struggle with literacy themselves. When children came to us at eleven, they were sometimes already far behind, and it was our job to try and help them catch up, despite how hard it was to bridge that gap. For all the kids who never took to reading, watching a child suddenly find pleasure in a book was the single biggest buzz an English teacher could experience.

Within my first five years of teaching, the teachers were dropping quicker than *Lord of the Flies*. Many of the friends I'd made in my PGCE training had left the teaching profession altogether, wrung out by the stress. A couple had moved to Dubai, some had moved to different careers, and one had crossed over to a private school. It was an unspeakable crime, only slightly less taboo than joining Only Fans. Katie had been my bestie during my teacher training and I was surprised to see her sell her soul to the devil, but she assured me she had made the right decision and that it had transformed her work–life balance – smaller class sizes, fewer behavioural issues and less marking. She tried to convince me that I was missing out, but as I heard her stories, I was never even tempted. A particularly dissuading anecdote she shared was when she had tried to tell off a student and he responded with, 'My father pays your wages.' I could cope with kids telling me to fuck off, but I don't know if I'd be able to cope with that level of arrogance from kids who happened to have won the fertilisation lottery. For me, the only thing that made the job worthwhile was the fact that my students valued the education they were receiving and the fact that I knew it genuinely had the power to change their lives.

Katie believed she was making a difference by educating students from the independent sector – and giving them some real-life knowledge about how the other 93 per cent of young people in the country lived. She was teaching *An Inspector Calls* when a charming young boy, Oliver, professed how Mr Birling was completely right to sack Eva Smith as she was 'clearly stirring up trouble and costing the company lots of money'. Oliver was the eldest son of an illustrious political family, whose academic achievement was mediocre at best, but he had the sense of entitlement that only comes from a privileged background.

Katie asked him whether Eva had the right to ask for a pay rise, just like Mr Birling was justified in thinking about his company's profit.

He reflected for a moment and then retorted, 'People should be happy with what they've got.'

Katie said, 'What if "what they've got" isn't a liveable wage?'

'Well, then she should look for another job and he can just replace her.'

Katie was a lot more dignified in her response than I would have been. She used the analogy of Oliver in his football team – hoping he would understand if money was taken out of the equation. She asked him how he would feel if his coach didn't pick him for the team, even though he was the best player, because he had asked to be captain. Before Oliver could reply, Katie added, 'And your best friend replaced you in the team, even though you were the better player, only because you asked for something you wanted and deserved – and then you got struck off the team for life.' Whilst Oliver was processing the analogy, she hoped the exchange had revealed something important to the whole class. But as she told me the story, I couldn't help but wonder if the message had sunk in at all.

Oliver went on to gain an offer from Oxford to read Philosophy, Politics and Economics, and Katie was quite stunned that he had managed to bluster his way through the interview with not much of his own merit to offer except his father's status, bank balance and contacts.

He was not an exception. I've seen first-hand how much is handed to private-school children without them realising it's a gift of privilege. I tutor children from across the social spectrum, and in the last year alone, when the pandemic led to the cancellation of GCSEs and centre-assessed grades were used to determine final results, I personally saw rich parents appeal their child's grades, convincing the head-teacher to write to the board saying they had made a clerical error. Their wish was granted – because they paid fees – so they were able to use their influence and power to literally buy their child's grades. Yet in our school, and many others across the country, genuinely gifted children were caught in statistic postcode discrimination, as their school had to match the previous years' results. Mr Wilson told me that Martyna, who was now in the sixth form, despite getting high grades from her teachers, was moderated down by the exam boards due to the school's previous data, and lost her university offers, including Oxbridge. She would have been the first in her family to go to university.

In my fifth year of teaching, our school became part of a scheme set up by a charity organisation. It offered teenagers from areas of high socio-economic deprivation and social immobility the opportunity to win a full scholarship to attend a top independent boarding institution for sixth form. Two students from our school would be granted interviews, and through that could potentially get their foot into a world that would have otherwise remained unexplored for them.

All teachers were asked to identify gifted and talented pupils in Year 10 who they thought would benefit most from this scheme. Those children wrote a letter of applica-tion, expressing their interest and explaining why they deserved the scholarship. The senior leadership team whit-tled the list down after considering target grades, effort and potential. By Year 11, the management had a strong idea of which students could be suitable candidates and those selected were assisted in filling out the application form and writing a personal statement. It was a long, arduous, but exciting process, with the promise of an unparalleled outcome for our kids. Yasser had transformed his work ethic and commitment, so I was delighted when he was chosen for interview at one of the most prestigious schools in the country. This school had a long list of reputable alumni, a high percentage of its students went on to Russell Group universities, and it had one of the two Olympic-size swimming pools in the country. All for a mere £42,000 a year.

Since those days of Mr Clarke driving Yasser to practice, we'd all become invested in his future. He was a gifted student, and there was no stopping him. He'd often return to my classroom after school and we'd go through his homework, or talk about extension tasks. We prepared Yasser to the best of our ability and organised mock interviews using standard questions covering favourite subjects, ambition, strengths and weaknesses, etc., but on the day of his interview, the headteacher asked Yasser something unexpected: 'You will be sharing a dorm with students who will have £5,000 watches strewn across the floor; how would that make you feel?'

Yasser replied, 'Not all of us have things handed to us on a plate – some of us have to work for it. A watch would only impress me if I bought it for myself.' He got the place.

The scholarship meant that Yasser would be provided with all the equipment and resources he would need in order to enhance his education to the highest possible standard, and to ensure he never felt at a disadvantage compared to other students. This included the money to buy new suits to wear, a laptop to use for work – and even his school trips were paid for.

He kept in touch with us, letting us know how he was getting on and sending news of his successes. As it was a new scheme, and we had got two students successfully in, Mr Thorne wanted teachers to visit the students to feed into the planning and expansion for the following year. I volunteered to visit Yasser along with Mr Clarke and we set off unto the fields and to the sky all bright and glittering in the smokeless air.

As soon as we arrived, Yasser was in the foyer waiting for us. He stood up, dressed in a well-fitted suit, and I noticed how grown-up he looked. He took us for a tour around the acres of hilly fields, cricket and golf courses, and inside, we were chaperoned through the theatre, multiple boarding houses and indoor riding arena. Where he once used to practise athletics in the local park, Yasser was now being trained by ex-Olympic coaches. I had never seen such a place in my entire life. It was like a fantasy. A bit like *Harry Potter*. Many of our children had hardly ventured outside Tottenham – but Yasser's last school trip was to Wall Street. If someone had told him two years ago that this was what his life was going to look like, it would be unfathomable – something he wouldn't have even imagined to be an option in his wildest dreams.

As this slightly familiar, six-foot-two boy sat with me in the canteen, excitedly sharing tales of the last year over some five-star cuisine, I watched how much Yasser had changed. He had a silent confidence, he walked differently and spoke with more assuredness. He had even become vegan.

The next time I met Yasser, I was sitting in the assembly hall with his mother and sister, after his school elected him to be Head Boy. The sixth form had invited a couple of Yasser's former teachers as a surprise for him. In the years we'd been teaching him, we'd spoken to his mother constantly, and we were still in touch as we guided his younger brother down the same path. Yasser arrived on stage to deliver his speech and he had the entire hall captivated. He was clever and articulate, funny and charismatic, but still retained all of his previous humility and charm. And that personality is something that cannot be tutored or bought or inherited. It comes from life experience and living in the real world. Watching Yasser on stage was an indescribable joy, and as his mother wiped her tears next to me, I was pretty sure Mr Clarke was close to crying too. Yasser's success exemplified how powerful the impact of resources and facilities can be, and the particular value they hold when they are given to children who appreciate them, deserve them and have earned them.

In our school, Yasser's story became an inspiration for the younger boys, and still is. His younger brother could see if he worked hard, he could have it too. He's now going to the same school, on the same scholarship.

After Yasser, our school gained more scholarship places. The better our students did in their scholarship schools, the more places were offered to us. The highest number before I left the school was twenty-one places – twenty-one students who would potentially get access into this alien world. The school began identifying potential candidates to put forward from Year 8, because it gave us more time to prepare and coach them. We didn't have the funding to hire new tutors, which would have been ideal to increase the students' chances of meeting their conditional offers, equivalent to what a private tutor would have done for those who could afford it. The places were heavily dependent on GCSE results, placing an even greater significance on exam success, so existing teaching staff voluntarily gave up time themselves and provided additional classes and tuition. We created a whole scheme of extra resources ourselves, and brought in alumni to help out with interview training.

As a result, we achieved our first ever offer from Eton – for a boy who, by all accounts, was extraordinarily gifted. As word spread, more children wanted a shot at these places – a legitimate, concrete promise of a reward for hard work. But despite the increase in the number of places offered, compared to how many students were fighting for them, they were still minimal – and therefore, the process to secure your place was incredibly rigorous and competition was fierce. The unfortunate truth was that the majority of students who put in three years of training would end up not making the final cut, even if they met all the requirements.

A couple of years after Yasser left, he came back to the school to speak in assembly and talk to younger students about his experience of boarding school. Everyone was absorbed by his anecdotes and buzzing at the thought that he was once sitting in the hall just like them, wearing the same blue jumper. At break-time that day, Angel was waiting for me outside my room. She wasn't amongst the highest achievers in her year group, nor was she the best behaved, but she was vibrant and opinionated and I loved that she had something about her. She said she wanted to ask me something, but seemed embarrassed.

'Miss . . . I, um, actually never mind.' She was about to rush back out of the room, but I stopped her.

'Angel,' I said. 'What is it?'

She twisted her hair around her finger nervously.

'I . . . er . . . wanted to talk to you about applying for a boarding school.'

She waited for me to laugh or show some sort of shock or horror.

'I think that's a fantastic idea,' I said. 'I'll add you to the list of students I'm going to put forward for the first meeting.'

Even though so many years have passed, I can still remember the way her face lit up at my response – at the thought that she too could see the world that Yasser described with her own eyes. At the thought that she could escape her house and her life and have a fresh start somewhere amazing.

And so began the metamorphosis – Angel's break-times, lunchtimes and after-schools were spent in the school library. Her work was completed. Her classwork was exemplary. Angel was often asked by her friends to join them, but she was on a different path. It was a unanimous decision that she would be in the final list of students whose applications were sent off to the schools, and she received a conditional offer from Yasser's school.

Results day is always terrifying. But it's even more terrifying when you know how much there is to gain or lose depending on what letters appear on that piece of paper. As Angel stood, holding her envelope, no family member with her, the paper was discernibly trembling. Ms Lewis stood next to her, and put her hand on her shoulder.

'You've done everything you could. And you should be so proud of yourself, regardless of what's on that paper,' she said. Angel nodded.

With a deep breath, she opened her envelope. She smiled, going through each A grade, one by one, screaming and jumping when she got to Science – the one she had been most worried about. And then she got to Maths – two marks off the A grade she needed to meet the offer for her scholarship.

The school sent off her exam to be remarked but the original grade was upheld and despite our best attempts at negotiating, they refused to budge, or allow Angel to retake Maths in November. All those years of hard work and sacrifice had been crushed in a second, because of two measly marks.

Angel's B grade was replaced by someone else's A – but a rich kid's A and a poor kid's B cannot be compared. Those two grades tell completely different stories and show completely different struggles. Angel wasn't extraordinary enough, but you shouldn't have to be extraordinary to get to the same place that extremely average children with elite parents reach easily. Both are held to completely different standards.

For the disadvantaged kids who went to our school, these opportunities were a make-or-break moment in their lives. These opportunities didn't come around every day, and they certainly didn't have their parents' safety net to fall back on if it didn't work out. In fact, many of them had to consider their family's needs before even starting to think about themselves. Just that one detail makes such a massive difference. And I know this because I was one of those kids who couldn't save up for a deposit for my first house because I was helping to pay my parents' rent. No one bought me driving lessons, or my first car, or paid for my insurance, or funded my travel abroad to increase my prospects. I had bills and responsibilities. My income was helping my family by offering them a little more comfort to return some of the love and care they had shown me. Perhaps that feeling is something that only immigrant children or working-class children will understand, but when you watch your parents sacrifice their lives, their country, their friends and family to give you better prospects, it means that you begin your adult life shouldering an immense responsibility to somehow repay them. And just that fact alone means you are starting the race with a handicap. The children we were teaching couldn't afford – literally and metaphorically – to take risks because there was no one there to fix it for them, or pick up the pieces, or call in favours. They had to make it on their own. That is the difference.

It is so easy to look from a lens of privilege and easily dismiss a child's story by hiding behind the myth that we live in a meritocracy and the answer lies in simply working harder. But actually, there are only so many hours in the day. And however frustrated I got sometimes, the blame cannot lie with parents either, many of whom are working tirelessly all hours of the day and night, in low-paid jobs, and trying their best for their children. They don't want pity, they just want equity, parity and a level playing field.

While at one end of the spectrum we were doing everything we could to help the brightest kids, we were also trying to cope with the political policies that wreaked havoc on the more challenging ones. When you have people who have never set foot inside a state school making decisions on their behalf, it is no wonder that the outcomes don't have the children's best interests at heart. You only need to look at the patterns of exclusions to see this in action. Mainstream schools and the local authorities are supposedly responsible for ensuring that all excluded students finish their compulsory education, but most ended up in APs (Alternative Provision) and PRUs (Pupil Referral Units). These are basically institutions where excluded students are sent in order to try and get an education. They are taught key subjects so they can leave with some qualifications, and are supposed to spend more time on behaviour sessions. The aim is to try and improve behaviour so students can return to mainstream education once they are ready. In theory, that's great. However, because very few schools want to take the responsibility of taking such troubled children back, they end up either dropping out, or staying in the units until they are at the legal age to stop attending school. Statistically, in certain parts of England, exclusion rates are also about five times higher for Caribbean pupils, which goes to prove the racial disparities that exist within the education system. And essentially, what this does is group all the 'bad kids' together into one confined space, where they can influence and deter each other, leading to less chance of reformation.

It's one thing to read about this information in articles and essays, but it's a whole other thing to see it unfold in front of your eyes. During the Christmas holiday in 2017, I was in bed, Netflix and chilling by myself, when my phone buzzed. I reached over to check it, and it saw a text from Aurea, where she had attached a news article. There was no explanation or message attached, so I clicked the link, wondering why she felt this was relevant to me at an hour that was well past both of our bedtimes. The headline described three teenage boys who had been convicted for the murder of an eighteen-year-old boy. They had knifed him to death outside his house after a disagreement over money escalated, resulting in the victim being stabbed four times. I read through the article, confused and horrified, reading the victim's mum's statement where she described her son as 'the light in her life that had been taken away from her'. The article outlined details of the trial and the judge's decision to give a life sentence to all three of the perpetrators. Good, I thought, scrolling back up to see the photo of the victim, a young boy, smiling at the camera with his mum.

As I got near the end of the article, there were three, smaller photos of the convicted murderers. Under their photos were their full names, which the judge had agreed to disclose to the public. There were two names I didn't recognise, and then I stopped at the third. It was the boy who had been carrying the knife and had committed the actual murder. I recognised the name.

James Amin.

I'm not sure how long I looked at that photo for. It could have been minutes, it could have been hours. I just stared at it, wondering how I didn't recognise him the first time I looked at it. I stared at it, trying to marry this image with the James I remembered. He had the same face, the same eyes, the same fluffy lashes. He looked the same . . . but different. His jaw was slightly more defined, his forehead had frown lines on it. He looked like he had been hardened. I looked at his face and thought about the times he had sat in my classroom, laughing and joking and getting told off. I thought about his parents' evenings, when he skilfully manoeuvred his mum over to me so we could gush over how much potential he had. I thought about Marvin and his GCSEs, and how one moment changed the course of these brothers' lives forever. I looked at his face and I thought about all the life he still had to live.

I couldn't reconcile the fact that the same James from my top set who I had fought to keep in school – the James with all the promise in the world – had taken another boy's life. I learned many lessons through my teaching, but the hardest one was that you can't save them all.

When I imagined a high-school killer, I used to imagine some sort of social outcast. A weird, silent teenager who teachers and students agreed always had something sinister about them. I didn't imagine a kid like James. I didn't imagine the kid who beamed when I gave him a smiley face on his work, the one who called his mum 'Mummy', the one who handed out the books for me and helped me tidy up and was shy around the girls he liked.

It begs the question, what on earth happened in the three years between James being excluded and him becoming a murderer? The statistics tell an alarming story: almost half the people in prison today were expelled from school as children, and about half the young people in young offenders' institutes were in care growing up. Has the government not spotted these trends? Of course they have. But it would take too much effort to change the system – so instead they ignore it. The government is so fucking busy obsessing over Brexit, while our kids are dying in broad daylight. They cut any funding going towards education, or the wellbeing of our young people and invest in pointless and meaningless initiatives that benefit no one but tick tokenistic boxes.

Education is a huge political football and each new minister, desperate for honour, tries to make huge upheavals to leave their mark. New initiatives and new changes to syllabuses, which are only implemented to show that 'something' has been done, leave teachers with the onerous challenge of updating all their schemes of work, resources, templates and records.

The Prevent initiative, which commenced in 2015, was a particularly egregious government horror show, where all schools were compelled to partake in a training day which aimed to protect children from the risk of radicalisation. Part of the government's plan was to help teachers understand the signs of student radicalisation so they could report any suspects as part of their safeguarding duties (as if they didn't have enough responsibilities already). I didn't know much about it at first, but we all entered the school hall just before the training was due to begin. Two white course leaders were setting up the presentation, whilst we all found our named seats on tables. Teachers are worse at following rules than kids sometimes and loads of them were trying to swap name cards around to see whether they could sit with their friends instead, just like a Pakistani wedding. I sat on a table with Ms Bloome, Mr Abara, one of the International Women's Day assembly teachers (a bit awks) and a couple of others. Little did I know, it was about to get a whole lot worse. Instead of talking about terrorism, the course leader played a game of 'how to spot a Muslim', pointing out what the government perceived to be typical terrorist traits. The list included, 'He will shout "Allahu Akbar"', 'He may have a beard' and 'He may wear a religious symbol like a crescent'. He basically described my dad. It was humiliating and offensive to be sat in a room as a Muslim teacher and then be expected to deliver this message to children too, many of whom were Muslim. As a result of widespread criticism, Prevent was adapted so it was more generalised – but the damage had already been done and, by many accounts, the initiative had lost all credibility.

Prevent was just a small window into how government and a certain section of society perceived some groups. As a Muslim I was hurt, and angry, but being in a school in one of the most diverse parts of London, the impact of such policies was even more brutally felt by both my colleagues and my students.

Institutional failures leave personal tragedy in their wake, which inadvertently affects our professional life too, and this was most noticeable when my friend Holly found herself and her family fall victim to the Windrush scandal. Holly was born in England and her family had lived here since the 1970s. In fact, her father was a teacher in the United Kingdom but made the mistake of going to his mother's memorial service in Zimbabwe. After landing back in the UK, he was denied re-entry and told he could not return to his family. The government wanted thirty years of proof that he had lived and worked here. But there was a catch: the Home Office said they would not seek out anything pre-digital, so it was up to Holly's family to find them. Aurea and I assisted where we could, taking turns to cover Holly's lessons, and Ms Lewis tried to free up Holly's time so that she could source evidence from so long ago. But then, the case received a massive setback: Holly's father was in a house fire in Zimbabwe and suffered a stroke as a result of the severe burns. Now, severely disabled and with his speech affected, the family was unable to continue their efforts without his guidance. In our free periods, we sat together and called solicitors and journalists and anyone who would listen – but to no avail. Holly then contacted her local MP, Jeremy Corbyn, who helped her to escalate her case at the Home Office. He personally wrote to the government, asking them to search their archives for records and his request was eventually granted, so we were all relieved and confident that Holly would have her dad home in the next few months. She was nearly there. But just before this could happen, her father suffered another stroke in Zimbabwe and unfortunately passed away. Holly didn't get to see her father again, or attend his funeral. Teachers are commonly told to be pro-government in schools; it is seen as a part of our role to teach young people to adhere to rules and engage with politics. But how do you convey a message to the kids with any real conviction, when you've been unprotected and let down by a system yourself?

As the school ricocheted from policy to policy while trying to manage budget cuts, the teachers and students grew more agitated. I saw the mood shift, and the sense of positivity diminish. This atmosphere culminated in an event organised at Westminster Abbey where pupils from deprived boroughs were being given the opportunity to get in front of, and even ask questions to, politicians, prominent journalists and activists. The purpose of the event was to help disadvantaged students engage more in politics and create dialogue between the politicians and young people. We selected a handful of students to take on the trip and they would be joining an audience of approximately 400 others from all around the country. Leyla, Ugur and Ojani from my class were in the group, and as we crept through traffic to central London I could hear them excitedly pointing out sights and chatting about the day ahead. I'm not going to say they were having a thoughtful political debate, but they were energised and curious. Sitting at the front with the rest of the teachers, it felt like this could be something meaningful.

As our kids walked through Westminster and inside the doors of Westminster Abbey, they went quiet. I'll admit it, even I felt that to be Mistress of Pemberley might be something, stunned by every remarkable spot and point of view of my surroundings. It was like walking back in time, albeit with 400 children in twenty-first-century uniforms, rolled-up skirts and low-rise trousers. As we sat down in the pews, a simmering energy went through the room. But when the MPs took to the stage, that energy disappeared.

The speakers droned on, sending the audience to sleep through their boring lectures that I would have never sat through if I didn't have to model engagement in front of my students. I tried not to think of the countless things I could have been doing instead with my time – watching *Love Island*, for example. The kids sat like robots and the atmosphere in the audience was completely subdued. There was the occasional pre-planned question quite obviously fed by the teacher, along the lines of 'What inspired you to become an MP?', but there was nothing to inspire genuine questions or conversation. During one of the talks, a female MP attempted to convince the students that they should vote, and assured them that her party cared about young people. But nothing she said showed a genuine interest in young people or spoke to the kids in a language they would understand. None of the policies were rooted in their interest. It was only when one female student from another school put her hand up and stood to ask a question that our attention was drawn back to the room. We all turned to look in her direction as the rolling microphone was taken to her.

'The reason why I don't care about the government,' she said, 'is because they don't care about me or people like me.

The only time they care is when they hear my name on the news because something horrible has happened to me.'

That spontaneous, raw, heartfelt moment revealed the strength of feeling that was hidden below the seeming apathy in the room. That was the only comment that day that felt true, from the students or the MPs, and we got back on the bus disappointed. The children started chatting and laughing as we pulled out of central London, but my mind couldn't leave the ornate abbey and the sense that the people with money and power didn't think much about where we were heading on the coach.

In my experience, the students felt disillusioned with politics because they knew that the only time their needs were discussed was when there was a riot or protest, or their name was associated with tragedy. I remember when my student, Kamari, put up his hand and said, 'Have you seen the new hotel they're building next to the retail park, Miss? It's proper posh, like a Premier Inn or something.' And after a moment of consideration, added, 'It's because they're trying to get us all out. They're tryna make the place look all nice and bring all the rich people in.' These students were aware of gentrification and already had the insight to know that they weren't wanted. I took my students on school trips to help broaden their horizons and watched people cross the road when they saw them. How can you tell children to aspire to be a part of a society that doesn't accept or respect them?

As a school, we fought constantly against a system that put certain children at a disadvantage. We helped the most able win places at schools with more resources, we worked one-on-one with the ones who were desperate to learn, and we did everything in our power to protect the ones at risk of falling out of the system. We did all of that while we battled for our own rights in society, and tried to preserve our sanity. We found a lot of tricks to get round the system, but more often than not, it felt like an impossible task. It was worth it though, for those children who did secure a place at university, or those who just managed to stay in school when it didn't seem likely.

My father always told me that education is one of the only ways to break out of the cycle of poverty and deprivation. And I saw that to be true with my own eyes during my time as a teacher. An education is the greatest form of modern-day alchemy, transforming the lives of ordinary people from all walks of life into something quite extraordinary. The more educated they are, the more keys they will hold to open the doors of opportunity that would otherwise remain locked or closed. In the words of Robert M. Hutchins, 'A liberal education frees people from the prison of their class, race, time, place, background, family, and even their nation.' In turn, a lack of education leads to ignorance, divisive views and lack of social cohesion.

That's why my interest in education was not purely academic – the meaning of giving these children an education was a lot broader than making them learn about Pythagoras's theorem or Shakespeare. I wanted to teach these young people about the importance of evaluating life, analysing people, reflecting on experiences and standing up for themselves. I wanted to give them the skills to be able to question what they saw around them, formulate their own opinions and shape their own identity.

I really tried to instil these hopes and dreams through little hints and comments here and there, introducing my kids to the life waiting for them out in the wider world. I often spoke about when they would go to university to subliminally normalise this pathway for students who were ambivalent, or didn't have that natural expectation drilled into them at home. It is difficult to aspire to become something if it is so far removed from your daily experience that you can't even visualise its existence. I showed them videos and pictures of past students who had succeeded: footballers, doctors, rappers and entrepreneurs. I wanted them to defy the system that was designed to hold them back.

Because the system may be broken, but the people in it aren't.

8

Parents Need More Help Than Anyone
(Even When They Don't Deserve It)

Autumn and winter are not my seasons. I am definitely a spring and summer gal myself. I don't like the dull, bleak, grey sky and I don't respond well to the freezing cold, as I'm plagued with circulation issues. So, in an ideal world, I would hibernate throughout those months and re-emerge when it's warm and bright again.

But because of all that adult stuff like rent and bills, I still had to lug myself to work during that depressing half of the year. It was dark when we arrived, and it was dark when we came home. Our truncated sunlit hours were spent cooped up in a classroom like inmates – and parents' evenings in those months made gloomy evenings even gloomier.

When I was a child (a particularly geeky one) I looked forward to my parents' evening all year. I know that sounds weird, but it was a massive event for the whole Baig family – my mum, my dad, my brother, my sister and my cousins all attended. Asian families do have the habit of turning up in multi-generational droves, and almost always in the most limited and restricted settings, for example hospitals, and then pretend they can't see the 'only two visitors at a time' sign. So in the same spirit, we took over all the available seating in a school hall as if I was going into an *X Factor* audition. When it was finally our turn, we all huddled in front of the teacher, my grandmother poised to take notes. Luckily, because of how hard I worked, it was usually good news. As the teacher gushed about how brilliant I was, my parents would beam with pride and my mum would pat me on my back with the promise of later rewards. My dad would flirt outrageously with my teacher, telling her that he is my mother's 'toy boy', clearly revelling in the attention. We'd leave each parents' evening chatting away about the school, happy all the way home to a big meal.

It was perfect. A moment that was just about me, a celebration of my hard work, but also a chance to show off my family. I was proud of us. Of how invested everyone was in my schoolwork, the way my parents were proud of me, and the simple fact that I deserved the praise. More than that, though, I was proud of the fun we clearly had with each other, and the pleasure we took in each other's company. I assumed that teachers loved parents' evening as much as I did.

But fast-forward ten years, and at the end of a full day of teaching, the thought of having to speak to an eclectic bunch of mums and dads for three hours filled me with dread. Especially because most of them wanted to share a never-ending analysis of their lives, and the October parents' evening was so near the start of term we usually couldn't even remember their child's name. By 6 p.m., we didn't have the brain capacity to have meaningful and purposeful conversations. Instead we had migraines, dry mouths and exhaustion, and parents were a huge obstacle to my fantasy about getting home and taking off my bra, eating dinner and getting under my warm duvet.

After six parents' evenings a year for several years, I knew the drill. I set up my desk with a big bottle of water, a packet of sweets, and a discreetly placed list with children's names and photographs on it. I wore my smartest, most appropriate clothes and put on my biggest and most welcoming smile. My plan was to get in and out of each conversation with minimal harm, to the child, the parents, and to me. I remembered what a big deal parents' evening was for me and my family, I knew I could turn the family's evening into a lasting, special moment – something they could talk about afterwards over dinner, and something that they would want to experience again. That's why I was extremely complimentary during my meetings with the parents, rewarding my good students through excessive praise and being a saviour for the night to the naughty ones. I did have an ulterior motive, because if yours was the only desk where they didn't get annihilated by a teacher, they'd be indebted to behave well for you for the rest of the school year. It may sound unethical and tactical, but it worked. Strategy is everything when you're a teacher.

The first student to shuffle over to my desk was Hassan, a quiet and shy boy in my set 5 GCSE class who had made leaps and bounds of progress since I first started teaching him. His father – a strong, older man who used to be a farmer in a small village in Pakistan – sat in front of me with an impenetrable look on his face. I started, as I always did, by asking Hassan how he thought he was doing in English. This was always a good way to open because it meant, if you did have something negative to report, the parent couldn't argue with you if the child had admitted it themselves.

'Umm . . .' Hassan mumbled nervously, looking down at his fidgeting hands, 'I think I'm doing OK.'

'Just OK?' I smiled encouragingly. 'I think you're doing more than OK.'

Hassan smiled, eyes still firmly fixed down, and remained silent. His father, just like his son, was looking at the corner of my desk, his hands clasped together, resting on his lap.

'Right,' I looked up to speak to his dad, 'I want to tell you, Hassan is doing incredibly well. He is a fantastic student. At first, because he's so quiet, I didn't know whether he fully understood the content, but his written work has completely blown me away. I cannot believe the progress Hassan has made in such a short space of time.'

Hassan's father nodded along, but didn't say anything. I continued, 'If Hassan continues to work this way, he will definitely pass English, and hopefully with a very good grade.'

Hassan's dad eventually looked up at his son and kissed his head. Hassan sat unable to look in his father's direction, as if he were trying to contain his own emotions, when the father burst into tears.

I had seen tears at a parents' evening, but they usually came from a contrite child, or sometimes a mother embarrassed at bad behaviour. The fathers tended to be either assertive and controlling, placid and uninterested, or just not there at all. As I watched this grown man sobbing in front of me, I was incredibly touched.

'I can't believe he will get GCSEs,' he said in between sobs. 'I never got to go to school. I can't believe my son will have GCSEs.' I watched him take his son's hand again, his face filled with pride at the mere promise of one GCSE. 'I want him to become a big man . . . a big man . . .'

He thanked me repeatedly and I assured him, with a lump in my own throat, that Hassan would become a big man one day and vowed to myself to have a sneaky peek at his course-work the following day. A little helping hand goes a long way. And as he stood up with his son, put his arm around his shoulders and walked off, I took a sip of my water and a deep breath, ready for the next person on the conveyor belt.

Across the room, I could see Mr Wilson was having a very different sort of evening. He was trying to speak to a mum about her daughter, who was in his GCSE class, whilst the younger sibling was running excitedly around the table. The younger sibling was Ethan, who was in Mr Wilson's form, and had been causing him problems all year. I could tell that because his own mother wasn't intervening, Mr Wilson was trying to hold back from telling him off. Ethan was a gorgeous little boy, with braids in his hair, a piercing in his right ear and way too much energy. He always wore his trainers to school, always got in trouble for it and spent a lot of time in the isolation room. As he treated Mr Wilson's desk like a roundabout, he tripped over his laces and knocked over Mr Wilson's water bottle, which landed directly on his crotch area. Mr Wilson looked mortified, Ethan's mum looked embarrassed and Ethan ran off before he could get into any trouble. 'Had a little accident?' I texted Mr Wilson, and as his phone flashed, he looked up to meet my eye, and seeing the stricken look on his face made me burst into a fit of giggles.

The next family to sit down in front of me was Ugur's, an irrepressibly cheeky and sometimes charming boy I'd strug-gled with all year. His family barely spoke a word of English, so he was translating for me. I greeted them and they smiled excitedly, clearly keen to find out how their son was getting on. I went through the same process, and asked Ugur how he felt he was doing. He told me he thought he was doing OK . . . but felt he could try a bit harder.

'How's that?' I asked him.

'Err . . . by talking a bit less?' he replied.

'Well . . . I actually agree with you,' I said, and turned to address his parents. 'Ugur is very bright, but sometimes he does get distracted.'

Ugur translated. His mother's smile got wider and she looked at me with an expression of gratitude.

I continued, 'He has a fantastic, positive energy but sometimes, that results in him getting excited too easily and talking too much, which then distracts the rest of the class.' His mum listened intently and I was sure her face would split any moment now. She put her hand to her chest and bowed her head down to me. Her husband merely nodded.

Confused, I turned to Ugur. 'As I'm sure you'll agree, Ugur, the work you're currently producing isn't to the best standard you're capable of. I know you can do even better, if you try a little bit harder.' Ugur nodded earnestly, then turned back to his parents. As he began to translate, his mum grabbed hold of my hand and started kissing it repeatedly. She touched my hands on her eyes and then kissed it again. Out of the corner of my eye I caught Ugur's smirk.

The devious little shit . . . this boy wasn't translating what I was saying at all. He was selling his poor mother all sorts of dreams in Turkish, and she was lapping it up.

I could have addressed the issue there and then – called a Turkish teacher for support, issued sanctions, etc. – but I was tired and his mother was so happy that I didn't have the heart to crush her spirit. Instead, I let her kiss me over and over again in submission, wrapped up the meeting and let them go home.

I noted Ugur's smugness as he thanked me and walked off, and made a mental note to deal with him the next day.

Over the years, parents' evenings brought a new significance to me as a teacher and that was to offer an insight into the wider lives of the children I taught. One thing became clear – apples don't fall far from tress, whether by nature or nurture. Meeting parents provided a kind of context that hours and hours of being in a classroom couldn't; nearly every single time a parent would sit in that chair in front of me, within seconds everything would become clear like a picture developing from film. Aurea called it 'assessing the gene pool' – where everything made sense about why a child was a complete monster in our lessons, or why a child was so shy and insecure, or even why a child was angelic. It was like finding the missing piece of the puzzle.

As I looked across the hall, I spotted Abdullah avoiding his subject teachers and weaving his father in and out of the row of desks. I laughed to myself as this was completely expected from the boy who avoided his own teachers during lesson times, let alone after school. I went back to ticking off the students who I had seen and counting how many were left. The next time I looked up, to my horror, Abdullah was guiding his father towards me, intent on disturbing my entire system. He pushed in front of one of my Year 10 students and sat down. I'd have told him to leave and go to his actual teacher, but he looked so painstakingly desperate for some good news that I decided to give his father two minutes of my time. Now, I've had my fair share of dads making inappropriate advances at me, but Abdullah's father clearly couldn't care less about what I was saying about his son.

While I talked the father through the upcoming English assessments and shared anecdotes about Abdullah's engagement in my lessons (that he shouldn't have even been in), he repeatedly called me 'Miss Babe'. Initially, I thought it was a mistake and tried to correct him, first by smiling politely and tapping my name card, and the second time clearly telling him 'It's Miss Baig, like a bagel.'

'Oh yes yes,' he smirked flirtatiously, 'Miss Baigel, I like bagel. Sweet like bagel.'

Suddenly, it all made sense. It was clearer than Maury's DNA test that Abdullah was this man's son. As tempting as it was, I rebuffed Abdullah's father's advances. I wasn't shocked by his outlandish behaviour and had heard and experienced plenty of stories where the parents had crossed the line. In fact, I know of one particular teacher who exchanged numbers with a mother in order to communicate about her daughter, but instead received regular nudes.

Now I'm no parenting expert, but as teachers, we do have the good fortune of seeing a huge variety of parenting styles and over the course of the years, you do get to compare (mostly through outcome) what works and what doesn't. In case there's any confusion in the matter, sending nudes to your child's teacher is never a good idea.

We did sometimes come across parents who would cross lines and lack boundaries. It was rare in my school, and certainly more prevalent in less urban areas where my friends were teaching, but on the infrequent occurrences where a mum would excitedly announce 'We're like best friends!', I had a strong impulse to reply, 'No you're not. You're her mother, Karen.' Don't get me wrong, I am all for allowing young people to fail, pick themselves up, make mistakes and learn from them, but as adults, we have a wider duty for their safeguarding. Maybe I feel this way because I am brown and my own mum and dad's preferred style of parenting was particularly Victorian, but when parents style themselves as buddies, children end up losing out on the parental figure that they so desperately need at their age.

On the other side of the coin, we had parents who were almost non-existent throughout their child's time at school. They'd ignore letters and phone calls, not turn up for meetings, and the child would rarely mention them. I always wondered how they could miss a call from school, or not return the call, knowing it could be an emergency. There was always a direct correlation between parents you actually really wanted to see at parents' evening and the ones who never turned up. The child would sit down by themselves, to hear their own feedback. I always found that really upsetting and made an effort to be uplifting and enthusiastic. I never, ever mentioned the elephant in the room – or the missing elephant. The only guidance these children had was in the hours they were at school, and if they had uncaring teachers, or fell in with a bad group, they were really in trouble.

Living at home meant that I'd leave parents' evening as a teacher and go straight to an evening with my parents. And each time it reminded me of my happy childhood spent revelling in the attention of my teachers, my mum and my dad. The longer I spent teaching, the more I realised how lucky I was.

In 2013, the government introduced performance-related pay for teachers, which basically meant that 80 per cent of your students in every single class needed to make a minimum of two levels of progress, and if they didn't, your pay wouldn't go up. But the big problem was that sometimes it didn't matter if you gave your last-remaining, only functioning kidney, the circumstances and context surrounding a child could prevent that progress. As many of the issues happened outside school hours, we felt like we were being punished. No matter how much value we added, no matter what we did, no matter how much power we used to roll the boulder up the hill, like Sisyphus, sometimes, we had to helplessly watch it roll back down and start all over again. Ultimately, we were dealing with human beings – not robots – and there were numerous factors that were beyond our control, and beyond the control of the children, which could lead to a single bad day in an examination hall.

There were so many factors that could result in a child going down the wrong path and parenting was just one aspect of this, albeit a significant one. Sometimes we dealt with cases of domestic violence, neglect and abuse, and more commonly, the more understandable mistakes like lack of discipline or applying too much pressure. Many parents had their own unresolved issues with trauma and mental health and years of no support, which they were trying to deal with as well as bringing up their children. Just as I learned how to teach children from working closely with so many of them, I learned about parents by observing the impact they had on their kids.

More than once, I saw children shout at and threaten their parents who sat helplessly, waiting for the teacher to intervene or help. It's no wonder that some kids don't respect their teachers when they get away with speaking to their own parents in such a disrespectful manner. Often, mothers sat in front of teachers genuinely frightened of their sons – and I always found that particularly difficult to witness. I taught a student who was always exhausted in the lessons, and when I contacted his mum, she explained that he had been playing on his PS4 all night, every night. She admitted that she couldn't take it off him because she was afraid he would hit her. In instances like that, the school would organise a home visit to confiscate the consoles themselves. It wasn't unusual for teachers to carry out home visits quite frequently – sometimes, parents would call the school, instead of the police, to help get their child out of bed in the morning, or to restrain them during an argument.

There came a point where I really thought I had seen it all. That nothing could surprise me anymore. But then I met Alex and Catrina's father, and my eyes opened to the sort of wisdom some of these children were receiving at home.

It was a peculiar case right from the beginning. Catrina was in my class and Alex, her brother, was a couple of years older, and they had both moved to the school halfway through the academic year. They were thin, downcast and incredibly shy children, and Catrina in particular looked like she was about to disappear. Unlike most of the girls in school, she wore no make-up, and her uniform was buttoned up around her like a coffin. She seemed sweet, though a little wary of me, and in amidst the chaos of a classroom, she stuck out like a sore thumb for her utter lack of confidence.

From the very first day her father met me, I could tell he hated me. It wasn't in my head; he truly made no effort to conceal it. The first time I went to say hello at the school gate, he refused to look at me, even as Catrina insisted how much she enjoyed our classes. From that moment, every time I spoke to him he made an expression like I was scratching my nails on a blackboard. He sat through the first parents' evening as if he were withstanding torture, while his wife and Catrina sat meekly beside him. He was a small, wiry man with a permanent scowl and gritted teeth. I'd been trying to build Catrina's confidence since she joined my class and she'd been opening up in the last couple of weeks, but she was a scrunched-up ball here. The sessions lasted only minutes before her father made his excuses and pulled them away.

The mystery was eventually solved when, the day after the parents' evening, he emailed Ms Lewis insisting that his child was not to be taught any form of religious or moral education by me. He said, 'his family were strict atheists' and he 'didn't want his daughter being indoctrinated by my extremist views'. Catrina was taken out from my class – not because he got his way, but because I found him quite frightening and my school wanted to protect me from this sinister man. But it didn't end there. A month or so after that, he emailed the head of year about his unhappiness with his children doing Religious Education; he then wrote another email blaming the school for his daughter's poor mental health.

In the months since she joined our school, Catrina had become increasingly depressed, and though I didn't see her very often, I heard from other teachers that they had seen cuts across her arms and wrists. Of course, we had to tell the parents everything relating to a child, and when Catrina's teacher contacted her father about her self-harming, he wrote the mother of all emails, making a formal complaint to the governors that the school was plotting to massacre his family and setting up evidence to frame him. It all ended as abruptly as it started after he pulled Catrina out of school, and his son was excluded shortly after by the headteacher for Snapchatting a video of himself burning the Bible. Divine justice in action.

Catrina's father was a horrific example of how racism and extreme views can perpetuate within families and filter through generations. When parents tell their children the earth is flat, or 5G caused Covid-19, it is their right to do so, but it's the school's obligation to raise those topics in class, bringing in counter-arguments, facts and other opinions too. As Holly always says, 'You can't leave the whole family to be stupid.'

You'd hope that the one place students would feel safe is in their homes with their parents, but sometimes it was their parents who made them feel unsafe. I have sat in front of mothers whose breath was smelling of alcohol and fathers who have punched their child in the face in front of everyone due to a teacher's negative feedback. I have even seen parents threaten teachers for 'picking on their child', telling them they will 'wait for them outside'. And sometimes, when you put every ounce of energy into a child, only for their parents to undo it overnight, the hard work and effort you had invested all seem futile.

Gulsen, who had grown up to become absolutely stunning, was no trouble in the classroom at all – but that was because she was hardly ever there. Her truancy was the result of a newly blossoming romantic interest and I'd heard from other students that she'd started a relationship with an older boy from a nearby college. As far as we knew, her parents were quite strict and traditional, but we didn't know much else about them. The school contacted Gulsen's family about her attendance, and not quite understanding the possible impact, they also mentioned the boyfriend. Her father appeared to sound very supportive, and said he would talk to her – but this didn't miraculously result in Gulsen's increased motivation in class. She attended lessons more but she still wasn't *present*, often surreptitiously texting under the desk.

To improve the literacy levels across the school, senior leadership introduced half-termly assessments to determine the reading age of all students. They were given a selection of extracts to read, which got progressively more difficult, and they had to answer some comprehension-style questions on them. The highest possible result was sixteen years and six months and this wasn't easy to achieve – I think many adults wouldn't get beyond aged twelve (I know because I secretly attempted some questions under a pseudonym account). I had high hopes for most of my class, and, shall we say, blind optimism for some of them. They were nervous for the most part, except for Gulsen, who sat the assessment half-asleep. She was one of the only students in the school who received the highest possible result.

The following half term, we re-tested the students to measure progress and I walked around the classroom during registration, desk by desk, handing out everyone's results on a small slip of paper. As I headed towards Gulsen's table and put her slip on her desk, she smiled sweetly but barely looked at it. She was staring straight ahead, in her typical daze. I casually paused, pretending to check something on my clipboard, and asked her quietly what her result was. She unfolded the slip, had a look, and angled it so I could see it. Of course I knew what was on the slip because I'd looked beforehand – it was sixteen years and six months.

'What book are you currently reading, Gulsen?' I asked.

'I don't read, Miss,' she replied.

'Hmm. Sixteen years and six months isn't easy to get, Gulsen. I don't know if I could get it.' I laughed and I got *something* from her. A smile. I felt like I was getting through to her, while the rest of the class obliviously shared their results with each other.

'The test was easy, Miss,' she replied.

I looked around the classroom where excited sounds of 'Raaaahh, she got fifteen years' and defensive sounds of 'Yeah, but I didn't try doe' and 'Bun reading, man' were swirling across the tables. She followed my gaze.

'I don't think they agree,' I laughed, and she took notice of the class's reactions. 'If you're getting sixteen years and six months without trying, imagine what you could do if you tried.'

She nodded – it probably went in one ear and out the other – and I moved on, hoping that at least some of it had been absorbed.

Closer to Gulsen's mock exams, I asked to see her revision notes. She didn't have any, as I had expected, so every lesson, I gave her a model answer to read. I knew it wasn't enough revision, but at least it was something. And she was bright enough to be able to understand the model answers enough to recreate them – if she turned up to the exams. Every morning, I reminded the class about revision sessions that the English department were running. After a few days, at 4.10 p.m., albeit ten minutes late, Gulsen was standing at the door of one of my revision classes. 'Someone's at the door, Miss!' one of the class shouted, and as I looked up, there she was, waiting for permission to enter.

'Come and grab a seat, sweetheart.' I carried on like it was no big deal. Secretly, I was ecstatic.

This breakthrough with Gulsen may not seem like a big deal on the surface, but it was huge. She enjoyed the revision class, I was hopeful she would come back for more, and with her level of intellect, the sky was the limit.

But Gulsen didn't come in the next day. Or the day after that. After a week of her absence, we found out that Gulsen had gone home that evening after the revision session and got into a big confrontation with her father. He didn't believe that she had stayed behind after school for extra revision and as a punishment, he had tied her against the radiator for hours. Once released, Gulsen had tried to run away with her boyfriend.

We were all shocked. I wish we'd taken the whispers about her strict father more seriously and prepared for what might happen. Instead, we assumed she was adequately cared for because he had seemed moderate on the phone. Of course, it became a massive social-services issue, and Gulsen was away from school for a bit of time while the authorities investigated the case. When she eventually returned to school, she was quiet and subdued once again. Not just academically, but all of the emotional progress we had made with such meticulous and thoughtful implementation was so quickly ruined. The last thing she would now be focusing on would be working hard at school or revising for exams, and for me, even contemplating how I would begin all over again was almost too difficult to envisage. This time, before I would get her back to the stage she was at, I would have to undo the damage caused by her father and only then be able to put the necessary interventions into place to get her back on track.

The truth is we made some mistakes with Gulsen. I wish we hadn't told her dad the reason for her truancy, and I wish we'd had more foresight in what his response might be. I wish we had made steps earlier to protect her from her father. But that's just sometimes how it is. Sometimes, you can move five steps forward with a child but at the end of the day, they go home and take ten steps back. You can spend months and months of working with a child, but the parents can quickly unpick and unravel all that work over-night and put you back exactly where you started.

As I watched more and more children impacted by bad parenting, I started to lose sympathy for the mums and dads. I felt like I wanted to get them all in a room and explain to them the impact of their behaviour. I was sterner at parents' evenings, and firmer on the phone when I wanted to get to the bottom of something. And I wasn't alone. All my friends who'd started teaching at a similar time to me had grown exasperated with parents and we all became less reliant on euphemisms and more frank with our concerns. If you have a child, it's your responsibility to care for them. End of story. Then something happened that taught me how complicated things can be.

Maya was a Year 7 girl in my school who lived with her mum and younger sister. She was chubby, with a very slight lisp, and great fun to be around. All her teachers described her as a pleasure to teach and she clearly got her positive attitude from a happy and close-knit family. Often at break-time, I would see Maya go to the fence separating us from the adjoining primary school to meet her younger sister. It was always amusing to see how excited her little sister was when she saw Maya, and how much she enjoyed showing off her 'older contacts' to her own group of friends. It reminded me a lot of my own relationship with my older sister. Maya's mother attended all her parents' evenings and when she heard stories about how Maya was getting on at school, she would listen with such eagerness and interest, with the same playful nature as her daughters. She loved hearing about "the English school life", as she called it, and clearly took a lot of interest in her child's education.

But during the summer holidays, after another spat with their landlord regarding overdue rent, the family was given an eviction notice and told to vacate the premises. With nowhere to go or no one to turn to, Maya's mum left her two daughters at home while she searched for a safe and affordable place to stay. She instructed Maya to look after her sister and wait for her return until she sorted something out. For hours, the children stayed at home obediently, but when their mum didn't return throughout the night, they became increasingly worried. The next morning, tightly holding onto her sister's hand, Maya knocked on her neighbour's door for help.

Social services were called for help, and by the time their mother returned that evening, her children had gone.

She tried to approach the police station immediately but they wouldn't tell her where her children had been taken to. They said that the case was now with the authorities, and she would have to prove that she was of sound mental state to be able to gain custody of her kids again. Maya's mum cried and explained to them what had happened but when that didn't work, she screamed and shouted. Her voice fell on deaf ears and she was given the officious response that allows for no deviation from the script and refuses to take into account any specific context.

The school was informed and within a few days, Maya and her sister were put into a foster home. They begged to see their mother – she begged to see them – but she had been deemed unsafe so any visits were prohibited to avoid confusing or further traumatising the children. Their mother had become extremely frustrated at the authorities and her inability to articulate her grievances didn't help her case. She verbally abused them, screamed, used profanities and even threatened to kill them. The more they didn't listen, the more she raged, and the more she raged, the more she played into their hands. They said she was mentally unstable and incapable of looking after her children.

The situation understandably escalated, with the children and their mother both becoming increasingly agitated. Maya and her sister decided that the only way to get out of the foster home and return to their mother was to run away. It was a cry for help – a desperate plea to be heard – but it had the exact opposite effect: the siblings, who at this point only had each other, were separated.

We followed the case from afar, but we could see the impact right in front of us. Maya was incapable of staying in a lesson without breaking down or working herself up into a fit of anger, breaking windows and causing mayhem around the school. For months, they told her that she could go back to her mother 'when the authorities finished investigating', or 'when her mother started her medication'. And after months of repeatedly being given false hope and being let down and disappointed, Maya tried to kill herself.

The social services diagnosed Maya with mental-health issues that rendered her a hazard to herself and others. They prescribed her a heavy dosage of medication, and what was left was a feeble girl walking around the school in a half-comatose state, looking like a shell of her former self. All she had wanted was to reunite with her sister and mother.

In that moment, she was desperate and thought her children would be safer at home than roaming the streets with her. What she needed most was a bit of time, help or at least a sympathetic ear. If she were more aware of how the system worked, she would have put on a suit or dressed smartly, and apologised to the social services and promised to do better. But she was raw, human and naïve. So, she shouted and screamed and demanded for her children to be returned to her and ended up losing them completely. And her children lost everything as a result.

In your twenties, you often see everything as good and bad and had I heard Maya's mother's story when I first started teaching, perhaps I would have been more judgemental of her actions. I'd no doubt have felt horror at the idea of anyone leaving two young children alone at home through the night, and I probably wouldn't have thought much about extenuating circumstances. However, there does come an unnamed, invisible hour that creeps up on you, when you stop seeing things in binary oppositions and begin to appreciate the subtle complexities in life. In the words of Harper Lee, 'You never really understand a person until you consider things from his point of view.' So many of these parents were a victim of the same system, who grew up with a distrust in the authorities. All I saw now was a helpless mother, two traumatised children, and rigid, unwavering authorities who were following policies with no attempt to adapt them to cater for individual cases. I saw a failed system that had failed everyone. As a teacher, you witness numerous travesties like this, and all you can do is try your best to help parents help their children by making the most of the limited interaction we have with them. My experiences with Catrina and Gulsen's parents taught me we had to be constantly aware of real threats, whilst what happened with Maya showed me that sometimes parents needed more support than children.

So, on a particularly cold wintry parents' evening, I ploughed ahead with appointment after appointment, giving my last dear fuel of life to each family. If I could make the parents feel proud, and the children hopeful, for just one evening, who knew what effect it might have?

Just as I was wearily looking at the clock, I noticed a slightly shy and nervous figure hovering awkwardly around me. Thankfully, it wasn't Abdullah's father. It was Mr Wilson.

'Would you like a lift home?' he asked, after the last parent left. 'I'm going that way to see a friend and can drop you on the way.'

Happily, I accepted the offer, knowing that this friend was possibly the same friend he had been coming to 'find' on his recent routine detours through the English corridor.

As we walked together towards the car, chatting away about the oddities we had encountered that evening, at the risk of cringing you out, I didn't even notice the dismal sky and didn't even realise that I wasn't wearing my coat.

During that drive, it took some prompts to get him to speak about himself, but eventually, with some sentence starters, we got there, and I learned more about his family. They were from Jamaica and he lived with his mother, sister and stepfather. When he talked about his family, I could see how close he was to them. His mother sounded like a remarkable woman, a real matriarch, who had been through a lot but had taught her children to not look inwards but give to others to gain contentment. There was no bitterness in his tone, no sign of any struggle. Just a man with strong faith who got on with it with what was possibly the most positive attitude I had ever come across. He was so laid-back, he was almost horizontal, but his stability was the perfect anchor to my energy and vigour. He loved his mum's cooking and his ex-girlfriend had cheated on him so the parallels were uncanny. When you know, you know. And I knew.

For the first time, I wasn't in an eager rush to reach home and get my hands into some rice and curry. I wanted this journey to continue, listening to this man talk about everything and nothing. I wanted to learn about his values which, at their core, were the same as mine. Family. Peace. Financial security. Freedom.

We arrived at my house and I reluctantly got out. He rolled down the window.

'Thank you for the lift,' I said.

'My pleasure,' he replied.

'If you put your postcode on to the TomTom, it will take you back to the High Road.'

'Don't worry. I done it already,' he replied.

Chuckling to myself, I walked up to the front porch to my family, knowing that spring had finally arrived.

9

You're In Charge of Your Own Destiny

Many of you have probably heard about Ofsted – and no, of course it doesn't stand for *Overpaid Fuckers Stressing Teachers Every Day*. For those of you who don't know what it is and what its purpose is, let me explain: nor do we. As far as I can tell, Ofsted is an organisation of inspectors who failed at being teachers themselves but wanted to stay within education, so now go into schools to make judgements about real teachers and how well they are doing, based on a random twenty-minute observation. All teachers are aware of the well-known adage: 'Those who can, do. Those who can't, teach. Those who *can't teach* become Ofsted inspectors.'

I only had the pleasure of experiencing Ofsted once in the entire duration of my teaching career. It was quite exciting really – in a picking-a-scab-and-seeing-if-it-will-bleed kind of way. I was in the middle of a lesson when an emergency message popped up on the computer screen, asking all teachers to meet in the staffroom at break-time. As we gathered for the announcement, it was clear from the management's solemn faces something serious had happened. Mr Thorne looked weary; he cleared his throat but not the worry in his voice, as he began the announcement. He told us that he had received the dreaded phone call that the school had success-fully dodged for the last eight years, and we were to be inspected the following day. 'Do what you always do,' he added, trying to rally his troops, 'and we will be GREAT!'

So, the whole school went into meltdown doing exactly what we didn't always do: the corridor displays were revamped; departments held emergency meetings to brief subject teachers on what evidence needed to be gathered; there was an emergency assembly for students, making behavioural expectations clear; and we were told that school would be open late for teachers to stay as long as they like to plan their lessons and resources, and of course catch up on marking, in case they were inspected.

See, this was their trick. Ofsted work on the basis of surprise, suspicion and secrecy. They don't tell you who is going to be observed, or which lesson, or which day. They usually call twenty-four hours in advance (though they have the power to turn up with no notice) and then a flock of grey-haired suited men arrive, who move from lesson to lesson like an ominous cloud. They remain completely impassive, aside from ferocious scribbling in response to the slightest indiscretion. And then they're gone, as quietly as they arrived, informing the school soon afterwards of their result. There are four Ofsted ratings: Inadequate, Requires Improvement, Good and – the holy grail – Outstanding. Once you get an Inadequate rating you are placed on special measures, constantly reviewed and threatened with school closure. We'd all heard about schools with an Inadequate rating, and the devastating fallout it created. There was little you wouldn't do to avoid it.

Of course, the lack of time to prepare is very much the point, so schools can't pull the wool over their eyes too much. But it means that as soon as you get the call, on top of all your other work, you have to plan the PowerPoint presentations, create resources, type up lesson plans outlining every activity and task with specific timeframes and objectives and ensure all seating plans are up to date for every single lesson for the next two days. And there is a good chance that it could all be for nothing – as there is a very small chance that an inspector would end up visiting your class anyway.

Despite my best intentions, I never turned into some sort of super-marker whose exercise books were always up to date. I still cut corners with some classes, let books stack up with others, and just buried my head in the sand some weeks. But I had got better, and more importantly, I knew exactly what to do in the event of an emergency. It was a sophisticated mixture of tactics: firstly, any students who were coming to the last few pages of their exercise books were given brand-new ones and their old books were locked away in my cupboard. That way, they would only have a couple of pages of work to mark by the end of the lesson. Secondly, I told one entire class to take their books home 'for a project' over the next two days (thanks for the inspo, Aurea!), and decided I would teach them some sort of debating lesson with a specially created booklet, and just show plenty of self- and peer-assessment and verbal feedback in the lesson. And lastly, I took the remaining pile of books home for my family once again to help mark. They loved me.

After a sleepless night, I woke up the morning of the inspection wired. I got to school bright and early and by 8 a.m., I was ready with the colourful stationery, Post-its, sorting cards and worksheets set on each table in perfect symmetry like I was hosting my first dinner party. As my first class lined up outside my classroom, I went out to meet them and we greeted each other with a formal nod and mutual understanding of the cause ahead. Standing nice and straight, they marched in, one by one, like soldiers, eager to make me proud. Across the length of the corridor, I could see the other classes doing the same.

We had established quite an effective routine over the year – the first two students in would hand the exercise books out for me, and everyone else got into their allocated seating plan and started copying down the learning objective, which was already displayed on the board. So we did what we always do. A smooth start. The students were excited – I was on edge – and overall, the energy was palpable.

As the kids sat silently writing, Tanya peeped up from behind her book, looked around to ensure it was safe, and then whispered, 'Miss . . . are they coming?' I looked around in the same way, like we were all detectives on a secret mission, then with my head up, strolled casually towards the door saying, 'I'm really glad you asked that question, Tanya . . .' in an unnaturally officious voice. I reached the door and peeked through the glass, confirmed that the coast was clear and then whispered back, 'Nothing yet! Corridor is empty.'

I shuffled quickly back to my centre spot, the class quietly giggling, and continued going through the starter activity, then the main activity, on to the plenary . . . all with my heart in my mouth and one eye on the door. The class behaved impeccably – any chance to show off. It helped that they liked me too. But as the lesson came to an end and it was nearly time for the bell, we were all quite disappointed and deflated. 'I wish they came. That was so good!' Farzana said, slamming her bag down onto the table as she packed up.

'I know, honey. Me too,' I replied. 'Maybe tomorrow. Make sure you behave in the corridors, OK?'

When the class emptied, I slumped into a chair and took a moment to close my eyes and breathe. I was sweating, and the inspectors hadn't even come yet. What would happen when they actually came? The anticipation was probably worse.

Dramatic as always, Aurea suddenly burst into my room with the urgency of a bank robber. Looking at the state of me, her hand flew to her mouth. 'Oh my God, did they come?' she whispered theatrically.

'No. But I'm sure this level of anxiety isn't good for my heart,' I replied, hand on my chest, my eyes still closed. 'I just want to get into my pyjamas and read some erotica.'

She laughed and patted my head. 'Oh, Baigy, you really need a shag.' I opened my eyes and looked at her with a mixture of surprise and outrage, and she giggled hysterically, while making obscene gestures on her way out of the classroom.

Another hour and another lesson later, I still had no visitors. What I did have was a splitting headache and multiple cups of coffee. Every time I thought I heard footsteps down the corridor, my body convulsed like a hamster under a defibrillator. The constant fluctuation of emotions was unbearable.

I was halfway through my afternoon Year 9 lesson, when I saw Ms Lewis's face at the door. I nearly vomited. In a state of sudden frenzy, I started to shout frantic instructions at the class, one eye on the door the whole time. Things I didn't even know the meaning of were spilling out of my mouth. 'FRONTED ADVERBIALS!' I gestured wildly to the sentences on the board. 'SPOT THE FRONTED ADVERBIALS!' My students looked equally as panicked. I briefly glanced at the door again and caught Ms Lewis grinning. She gave me a thumbs-up signal. This was it, I thought. I couldn't breathe. My voice was wobbling and my whole body was shaking. I was going to have my first Ofsted inspection! The kids sat bolt upright. I kept my eyes firmly fixed towards them, not daring to look at what was happening to my right as I heard the groaning of the door opening slowly.

'GOTCHA!' Ms Lewis howled.

In confusion, I turned to see Ms Lewis laughing hysterically, doubled over, hands grabbing her belly.

'Ms Lewis! How could you?' I exclaimed, too stunned to even laugh.

'Ah, girl. It was too hard to resist. Anyway, you don't need those old fools to tell you anything!' she said, and then turned to face the class. 'Keep up the great work, guys.' And just like that, this firecracker of a woman was gone.

On the final day of the inspection, I had come to terms with the fact that I wasn't going to be observed. Perhaps it was for the best. What did they know anyway? I knew how hard I worked as a teacher – what I did for my students day in and day out – and no twenty-minute observation could tell me otherwise.

I had made it to the last lesson, and was relieved that this anxiety-inducing nightmare was finally coming to an end. I perched on the end of my desk, utterly shattered, and decided I was done with teaching for the day. It was probably too risky to chuck on a video, so instead, I divided the class into groups and allocated each of them a scene to re-enact from *Of Mice and Men.*

'Mum – I mean Miss – can we make it modern?' Ugur asked.

'You can do what you like, my dear offspring,' I paused as he smirked cheekily, 'as long as each character says at least two exact quotes from the book.'

The class continued rehearsing and I twisted my feet out of my heels watching them: the bossy ones took on the role of the director, the quiet ones found their own silent roles, like the tree or the rabbit, and I felt relaxed for the first time that week. Who cared about some silly old inspector and his dumb observation?

'Please don't forget – no backs to the audience!' I instructed, wriggling my toes around so they got some sensation back into them. 'You have two minutes left and then it's performance time!'

And just then – just as I had thankfully squeezed my feet back into my shoes and was making my way to the back of the classroom – I heard that familiar groaning of my door once again.

Abruptly, I turned to see Ms Lewis standing at the entrance of my classroom with a solemn-looking old, white, bespectacled man standing behind her. It was the last twenty minutes of the last lesson of the last day – were they actually having a laugh?

I couldn't read Ms Lewis's expression – what was that? Worried? Apologetic? She walked in, leading the inspector to the back corner of the classroom. The room was strangely silent compared to the chaos a second ago. I'm pretty sure we were all holding our breath as we watched them manoeuvre their way through the crowds and to their seats.

'You can continue, Miss,' Ms Lewis prompted, her eyes wide.

'Oh . . . um, yes, of course.' Grow up, Mehreen. 'Right!' I clapped my hands. 'Can everyone take a seat . . . um, take a seat according to the SEATING PLAN,' I added a bit of extra emphasis, to make sure the inspector saw I was meeting the checklist, 'and group number one, whenever you're ready, the stage is yours.'

I glanced nervously in the inspector's direction and saw that he was scrutinising my lesson plan, flicking through the pages. He was clearly confused as drama performances were not listed anywhere on the list of activities. I tried to cover my back as best as I could. 'So at the start of the lesson, we realised that we were not perhaps as confident as we should be with the key quotes we need to memorise from the novella. So please remember the SUCCESS CRITERIA – I expect to see at least two key quotes from each character. And audience, remember your PEER-ASSESSMENT skills, I want you to tell me "what went well" and an "even better if" whilst you're watching, please.'

Group one took their positions, visibly terrified, and Ugur came to the front, fiddling nervously with his sleeve. Whatever was going to happen now was in God's hands.

'Whenever you're ready, sweetheart.' I gave him my most encouraging 'You've got this' wink. *Come on, Ugur, do me proud*, I secretly willed the universe to be in my favour, for once.

Ugur cleared his throat. 'Ladies and gentlemen . . .' he began, arms outstretched. 'Welcome to . . . *Of Mice and Mandem*.'

What the fuck? *Of Mice and Mandem*? As the class all clapped, I looked in utter horror towards Ms Lewis, who actually looked like she was stifling a laugh. I could see the tears brimming in her eyes. The inspector sat next to her with an unreadable expression.

'Take off your hood, Lennie. The weather's roasting.' Ugur was clearly excited as it got towards the climax of the scene. Spontaneously, he decided to introduce props into his performance. He pulled out his wide-tooth comb from his trouser pocket, pretending it was a gun, and put it to the back of Lennie's head.

He stared at his target intently. There was a moment of deafening silence.

'Pew pew!' He accompanied his shooting action with some award-winning sound effects. 'Pew pew!'

The class erupted into laughter and applause, Ugur was bowing, soaking in the adoration from his audience and I didn't dare to look towards the inspector. We got through the feedback and moved on to the next group – thankfully, there wasn't much time left. As I dismissed my class, Ms Lewis and the inspector thanked me for my time and left.

In the English office, I retold the story to my colleagues, who were in absolute hysterics, only exacerbated by my shame. I put my head on Ms Bloome's shoulder, and she held my hand as all the other teachers made jokes at my expense. 'What did the teacher do when Ofsted came into her class?' Aurea cried, tears streaming down her face. 'Pew pew!' And that was it, she was on the floor again.

When I got home that evening, Ms Lewis called me. I expected her to roast me about my lesson too, but she actually sounded like she was crying. 'Ms Lewis, is everything OK?' I asked.

'We got Outstanding in all areas,' she said in a quiet voice which revealed how unusually overwhelmed she was. 'The only school in the borough. Outstanding in all areas.'

I was quiet on the end of the phone too, in part because I was so happy, in part because I was so amazed I hadn't derailed the whole thing with *Of Mice and Mandem*, but also because I was so touched by the phone call. Ms Lewis was the person I'd admired and learned from. She was the person I'd gone to when I wasn't coping, and over the years, she'd always offered me support and guidance. I thought she saw me as a child, but that I was the person she called with this news showed that wasn't true. At least not any more. Even if I still thought I was twenty-one in my head, she saw me as an adult, a colleague, a friend, and that left me speechless.

The more confident I became in my teaching, the more I was able to be myself outside of the classroom. I used to hate speaking in the staffroom and I avoided social events like the plague, because I knew I would end up desperately trying to think of something valuable or funny to contribute and it would almost always go wrong. Whereas now, I went to the pub on a Friday, and sat with different teachers at lunch. My walks with Aurea started feeling like a social occasion, as they always involved stopping to chat with teacher after teacher. I made jokes and people laughed. It had taken most of my twenties, but now I felt less self-conscious and more secure in who I was and what I had to offer. Together, we built a network of genuine friends, and I finally could call myself a 'real' teacher.

I learned tricks and tips from other teachers, from how to get around marking, to how to deal with that particular boy in Year 9 who wouldn't take his hands out of his trousers. I also learned, *very* clearly, that teachers are people too. They make mistakes, they break the rules, they rebel. And because of how many hours they spend in school, a lot of those misdemeanours happen within working hours.

Schools are massively incestuous: everyone's shagging each other, talking about shagging each other, or reminiscing about that time they shagged each other. The science technician's room is a popular spot for these illicit encounters, but any abandoned office usually does the job. I vividly remember one of my friends having an ongoing, exciting affair with a really hot PE teacher. She would excitedly share the frisky tales of their hot and steamy affair, including all the intimate details, and we would all live vicariously through her. Two weeks after their latest rendezvous, we all sat in a staff briefing and Mr Thorne displayed a large, colourful photo of said teacher's wedding – an event that took place a couple of weeks ago. All the staff clapped and congratulated him whilst we exchanged horrified glances amongst ourselves. I learned a lot about men and marriage during my time in that school.

When I'd started, I'd known nothing about boys and men, but after a few years I knew more than I wanted to. So many men showed off their wives and children as their WhatsApp display pictures and swore they loved them – and they probably did – yet I knew they were shagging colleagues at work, and they were effortlessly able to separate the two. It was like work and home were two different existences, and their home wives were completely oblivious to their 'work wives'. By now, I had seen so many of these affairs that I was beginning to get quite immune to them and although I couldn't completely put myself in such a situation, I could see how spending so much time with someone could lead to an intimacy being formed. Perhaps it was the excitement of it being forbidden, or just the fact that everyone was too tired to have sex when they got home and therefore relieved themselves at school, but either way, I kept in a wide orbit of Mr Wilson.

Over the years we'd got closer, but never at the pace other teachers seemed to hook up. Perhaps it was my upbringing, or how busy I was, but something always kept us at the Flirty Friends stage. As I watched so many of my friends get into Dangerous Liaisons, I'd started to feel safer keeping it platonic. Even though he gave me butterflies when he dropped by with some chicken wings, or stopped me in the corridor for a conversation, who knew if he was equally unable to keep it in his pants and what he would get up to given half a chance? But the truth was, he seemed different, and with no free time to meet somebody, having a little cheeky banter at work was hugely convenient.

Despite my years of mixed messages and commitment issues, Mr Wilson was consistent with his interest and thoughtful gestures, without demanding anything in return. His attention didn't waver, even when I behaved like a fuck-boy. Dropping me home, bringing me lunch, coming into my classroom to speak to a student about 'something important' – all of these things had become a regular occurrence between us. And besides the fact that his benevolence was saving me a lot of money on Ubers and Deliveroo, it was a lovely feeling to know that someone was thinking of me. They were tiny gestures – sometimes just simple spicy wings left on my desk during a bad day – that proved something so much bigger, that someone cared about me and my endo-metriotic belly, and that someone was looking out for my welfare. People had started to notice and rumours had started to spread around the school, but I didn't really give it much thought. Mr Wilson gave me a brand-new motivation to dress up every morning, put on my lipstick and my heels on the dullest days and made me look forward to break duty. He brought logic to my unruly imagination and stability to my sass. Plus, I was nearly thirty, even my students were getting married before me, and though his grammar did leave a lot to be desired, I didn't want to die alone. Anyway, it was just a bit of fun – perfectly safe – or so I thought.

The lead-up to the GCSE exams was always incredibly stressful for everyone involved. It was busy and high-pressured and there was no time to slack. Everything these kids had done since primary school – all those years of hard work and early mornings and timetables and homework and revision classes – it all built up to this. The last couple of weeks of April were always mayhem – students were devotedly revising in my classroom at all hours of the day, we were marking and returning essays back and forth like a clock pendulum, piles of practice papers were being printed, photocopied and distributed, and even those who had never written an essay in their lives were now making flashcards – it was like everyone suddenly realised that the day that always seemed so far away was nearly around the corner.

Each year, by this point, my desk always ended up looking like a bomb site and dried-out highlighters were overflowing onto the floor. These were the months that you would find me wearing flats and with hair scrunched to the top of my head, in what Aurea used to call 'The Pumpkin'.

It's a strange feeling when you watch the children you first met as nervous eleven-year-olds talk you through their future plans as sixteen-year-olds. Over the years, you see them stretch out, grow facial hair, come into their own personalities, and hopefully become more confident young people. When the first students I'd taught came to me for help with their English GCSEs, it almost made me feel old.

On the morning of the English exam, we organised a 7.30 a.m. masterclass. This was so that we could give everyone a healthy, filling breakfast, cram any last-minute revision and calm any nerves. It also ensured that even if anyone were late to the masterclass, they would definitely be on time for their exams. I always brought some almonds from home that Mum had soaked overnight and we had peeled together in the morning, because that's what she used to give me before my own exams, claiming it would make my brain stronger. I'm not sure if that's a Pakistani thing, or if there is any scientific evidence to support this, but I made the students who didn't have nut allergies eat them before they went in. Even if it had a placebo effect, it was worth it. Everyone else got a banana.

Regardless of who the students were – how naughty, brave, feisty or studious they had been for the past sixteen years – on the morning of the GCSE exams, you saw them for what they really were: kids. There was a real vulnerability to them – an innocence that was visible in the panic on their little faces. I spent most of the two hours making dad jokes to try and lift their spirits. Abdullah's year were so nervous that it reminded me of their first day in Year 7 again. The same innocence. The same little faces.

'I done five hours of revision last night, Miss,' Abdullah said.

'I did,' I replied.

'Did you as well?' Abdullah asked.

'No, sweetheart, it's "I did", not "I done",' I said.

I thought he might smile or call me the 'grammar police' but instead he drifted away, absorbed by his thoughts. I knew it was time to bring out my inner Les Dennis to ease the tension.

'Right, pens down, please!' I said. 'I want someone to tell me: what is grammar?' I scribbled the question onto the whiteboard. A succession of hands flew into the air. 'Ayce?'

'It is using the right words and tenses and stuff. It's worth 4 marks in the literature paper.' That went on the board.

'Anyone else? Hassan?'

'Bad grammar is saying things like "I done".'

I smiled.

'OK, copy this down for me. Grammar is . . .' I turned back to my whiteboard and scribbled, 'the difference between knowing your shit and knowing you're shit!' It took a second for the lightbulb moment to come, but once they got it, they practically fell out of their seats they were so excited at the fact that their teacher had just sworn, and momentarily forgot all about the monumental task that lay ahead.

The masterclass would always culminate with me telling the students how proud I was of them, and how their success could not be measured in one measly exam, and then I would hand them personalised cards that I had spent the week writing, and then almost cry and do that ugly thing when the sides of your lips start drooping down. And all the kids would jump onto me in a giant bear hug. As they got into a single file and started making their way out of the classroom door, there wasn't much between them and the real world. I was simultaneously excited and terrified for them.

It's always weird saying goodbye to people you've seen nearly every day of the week for the last two years when you don't know if you will ever see them again. You watch them leave and a small part of you always wonders what happened to them next.

When Year 11 leaves for study period and exams, it's officially time to let our hair down. We finally have an extra couple of hours a week to chill out. I called it the 'winding down, waiting for the holiday' time of the year. The absolutely best gift was if you taught Year 11 for a double period after lunch and ended up with the whole afternoon off after they left, so as soon as it was lunchtime, you could relax for the rest of the day. One lunchtime in the post-exam summer term, Holly and Aurea came into my classroom, looking conspiratorial. 'Baigy . . .' Aurea said, 'we have a proposition for you.'

'Whatever it is, I'm not involved,' I recognised that devious look all too well.

'No – it's really good. I swear! Just hear her out!' Holly pleaded.

I raised my eyebrow dubiously and sighed, waiting for Aurea to continue.

'The weather is stifling!' she announced theatrically, pointing to the window, 'and it is against our human rights to be locked indoors.' She was ridiculous. 'Therefore, we believe we should make the most of this country's limited good weather and go swimming. Now.'

'Am I missing something?' I asked, scandalised by their behaviour. 'It's schooltime. We are literally at work.' I looked at Holly, who was laughing and already had her car keys in her hands. 'I expected this from Aurea, but Holly . . . you?!' The two of them fell about laughing again and I couldn't help but join in.

'Oh, come on, you little goody two shoes. Hurry up, we have exactly fifteen minutes before Ms Kowalski is back in her office!'

My protests melted in the breeze and before I knew it, we had made an impromptu escape plan. We sneaked out, one by one, like naughty schoolgirls, and met by Holly's car.

'Adios, suckersssss,' Aurea whispered, doing a wanker gesture towards the school. Half-terrified of getting found out, and half-thrilled at the rebellion, we let Holly drive us to the high road, purchased three bikinis, and spent the afternoon swimming around in an outdoor pool, like we were young again, without a care in the world. Naughty, I know. But peer pressure is a bitch.

Right when things had calmed down at work and I felt more relaxed, Year 11 prom tickets went on sale, creating a new buzz. I never went to my own prom (I wasn't allowed) and last year's disastrous prom night ended with me leaving early because the spitty French teacher got a bit too drunk and kept trying to grind on me, until Mr Thorne furiously intervened and escorted him out of the hall. So prom hardly registered in my mind, aside from the near-euphoric excitement of the Year 11s, who lost all focus in class while they planned outfits and discussed dates. That is, until Mr Wilson poked his head around my door one afternoon, looking even more nervous.

'Er, Miss Baig, quick question,' he said, still with one foot out the door.

Don't pursue it. Don't pursue it. Don't pursue it.

'Ask me anything.' My raspy voice and my fluttering eyelashes betrayed my intentions before I had a minute to think.

'Would you, er, go to prom with me?'

It was a faint, incoherent mumble, and I wondered if staff dates at proms were a thing, but my fanny had a mind of its own, somersaulting, not fluttering, as I watched him look down shyly.

Gripping the bottom of the seat so I didn't jump up too excitedly, I managed a cool, 'That would be fun, sure.'

He smiled, nodded, smiled again, and disappeared, leaving me to relive the memory in my head for days.

Suddenly I knew how the girls in my class felt, as I bought a brand-new dress and started preparing for his declaration of love. The dress was the most expensive one I'd ever bought, and probably over the top considering I was a teacher, but in the words of Oscar Wilde, 'If I am occasionally a little over-educated, I make up for it by being always immensely over-dressed.' I swapped some bits around in that to capture my motto: If you flash him, then you'll smash him – a more vulgar version of Wilde's profound thoughts.

Mr Wilson planned to pick me up from my home at 6 p.m., probably assuming I was a normal adult, but in order to avoid him being scarred for life after a potentially traumatic and possibly violent interaction with my father, I decided it was best for him to meet me at the top of my road. I waved goodbye to my family, donning a cardigan over my dress as I surreptitiously exited, because my mum didn't like my shoulders on display. Obviously, I quickly discarded it as soon as I saw him turn the corner and into my road, just as I did when I was seventeen. By the time Mr Wilson arrived looking like a snack in a navy-blue suit, I looked like I could teach torches to burn bright. It wasn't the first time I had been in his car but something felt different. The changing dynamic of the relationship made me feel a bit shy, as compared to my usual incorrigible self. I got into the car, he told me I looked beautiful, I told him my left side is usually my good side, and off we drove.

Upon arrival at the hired venue, the décor was magnificent. Yellow and gold balloons adorned the entire hall and there were rows and rows of delectable food and drinks. My friends were a bit too excited to see Wilson and me arrive together, and were behaving in a particularly uncouth manner, making dirty innuendoes at every given opportunity, like describing how big the sausages were, or asking whether he found it hard to get in – but luckily, he was far too decent to fully comprehend the extent of their vulgarity. Despite their best attempts to sabotage my new romance, I found myself having a really good time. Mr Wilson wasn't the 'party animal' type – he stood at the side and clapped, like my mum does at weddings. I, on the other hand, after about ten minutes of initial pleasant niceties, was in the middle of the dancefloor, giving an extra little wiggle every time I thought Mr Wilson was looking.

After hours of laughing, dancing and singing tunelessly over loud music, we trudged off the dancefloor, our feet aching. I took a seat and a soft drink, allowing my numb toes to rest, and ready to watch my kids dance the night away. I could just make out Abdullah in the distance, nervously dancing next to Ayce, edging closer and closer towards her. But then, almost as if he had second thoughts, he suddenly changed direction and rushed away from the dancefloor. I scanned through the gaps and saw him move towards the corner of the hall where all the bags and coats had been discarded. Facing the wall, he picked up his pouch and then reached deep inside it. What was he up to? Before I had a chance to get up and interject, Abdullah pulled out a giant bottle of Victoria's Secret body mist and sprayed it all over himself.

I was having such a great time; I didn't want the night to end. But like Cinderella, I had a midnight curfew and Mr Baig would no doubt be waiting up for me, so I thought I should go home and get some beauty sleep. There were enough other teachers to keep charge.

I was just about to call an Uber when a slightly out-of-breath Mr Wilson caught up with me.

'Mehreen,' he panted, 'I can drop you home. I'm . . . leaving too.'

'Let me guess. You happen to be going that way, in the complete opposite direction to your home?'

He made a face that said 'guilty'. As we went out to his car, I realised I hadn't stopped smiling with every step, and just before we got in he turned to me and put his hand on my arm.

'Miss Baig. I mean, Mehreen, I like you. Perhaps I haven't made that clear enough, but I really, really like you.'

I looked up into his kind face, felt the strength of his arm on mine, and knew I really liked him too. I, however, was somehow unable to speak. Looking into his sincere, brown, gorgeous eyes, all I knew for sure was that I was in exactly the right place.

The next few months with Mr Wilson passed in what can only be described as a state of pure bliss. He dropped me home after school every day, put the heater on in his car, and I fell asleep, all snuggly and warm, dribbling from the side of my mouth.

They say you should never date an English teacher, and they're probably right. We're bloody hard work. Not just because we're constantly correcting your grammar, but we also can't help but analyse every word you say with multiple interpretations. Like all teachers, we can be patronising, because we're used to dealing with children, and we do tend to moan more than Myrtle. But Mr Wilson put up with it all with a gentle smile on his face. Not once did he blame me for being tired, or hungry, or moody. I was fed and watered and incubated and I felt like the happiest plant alive.

It took a long time to get there, but I finally felt like I was in control. Sure of my abilities as a teacher, and finally sure of my feelings for Mr Wilson. But of course, no rose comes without a thorn. Just before the end of the school year, a new internal role was advertised in the school bulletin, inviting us to apply for Head of Year. This was an important pastoral role, and a key stepping stone for regular teachers before they could be considered for middle management. The candidate specification required someone who was able to develop the whole school reading drive (check), monitor student behaviour (check), implement appropriate interventions (check) and model and exemplify appropriate conduct at all times, including language, attire and professionalism (not so check, but whatever). I filled out the application form the minute I saw the vacancy and rushed to Mr Wilson's classroom to tell him the exciting news. He was going to be so proud of me.

I eagerly reached his door and leaned against it. 'Knock knock,' I murmured melodically in my most seductive voice. As I entered, I noticed he wasn't alone. Ethan was standing next to him, head down, hands by his side, doing his best to look ashamed. I waited at the side of the room for what seemed like a really intense discussion to finish.

'It's embarrassing for me, Ethan,' Mr Wilson was saying. God, he was hot when he was angry. 'I can't keep standing up for you and you keep letting me down. It makes me look

silly in front of the other teachers. Do you understand?'
Ethan nodded. 'What did I just say?' Mr Wilson demanded.

'You look silly in front of the other teachers when I let
you down,' repeated Ethan, rubbing some imaginary tears
from his eyes. 'I'm really sorry, Sir. I didn't mean to let you
down.'

Mr Wilson, being the big, muscular softy he was, relaxed.

'Off you go, Ethan. Please think about this conversation
tonight when you go home. I know you can do better.'
Ethan picked up his bag to leave and spotted me as he
turned. Instantly, he forgot he was supposed to be sad.

'Sir! Your girlfriend's here!' He turned to Mr Wilson and
made a massive smooching sound.

'Ethan!' Mr Wilson shouted, but Ethan ran out of the
room before he could get into any more trouble, chuckling
delightedly to himself. I laughed at Mr Wilson's weary
expression. That boy really was draining him.

'Hey,' I said, walking towards his desk.

'Hey . . . Can you just check my spellings in this form,
please?' he said distractedly, jabbing away at the keyboard.

'Of course.' I walked in, the news catapulting in my belly,
just bursting to come out. 'What is it? Let me have a look . . .'
One look at the screen and I knew I recognised the form. It
was the same form I had been filling in just two minutes
ago. 'Oh! Umm . . . so . . . you're applying to this?' I hesitantly asked, wondering how on earth I hadn't foreseen this.

'Yeah . . . I've always wanted to be Head of Year,' he
replied.

'How funny!' My voice was unnaturally high. 'Haha.
Umm . . . do you know what's really funny?' Mr Wilson
looked at me quizzically.

'What's wrong?' he asked.

'I just applied for the same job.'

There were a couple of seconds of silence, and then Mr Wilson smiled. 'That's pretty cool.' And then, as if he had just considered something else, he said, 'Would you rather I didn't apply?'

'No! Of course not!' I said. 'I just . . . I dunno. Isn't it a bit weird?'

'Not really,' he shrugged. 'More chance of one of us winning.'

I decided if it wasn't a problem for Mr Wilson, then it wasn't a problem for me. The invitation for interview came through the same day, and I had three days to prepare. I started typing up some brief notes about why I wanted the job, why I felt I deserved it and my vision for the future. Every now and then, I texted Mr Wilson and asked him if he needed any help preparing – just to be supportive and let him know that he shouldn't feel threatened by my brilliance.

The day before the interview, Mr Wilson came up to my classroom to drop off some hot wings.

'Hey . . .' I said, smiling gratefully. I was starving. 'Do you know how many people have applied for the role?'

'Twelve, apparently,' he replied.

'TWELVE? That's loads!' I exclaimed. 'Do you know who?'

He laughed.

'It doesn't matter how many people are in the running, or who you're up against, Mehreen. All you can do is be your-self.' God, he was so much like Buddha sometimes, it was bloody annoying. Trying to provoke some sort of reaction out of him was like getting blood from a stone. 'But . . . I did hear Lever and Clarke talking about it yesterday, so I know they've applied.'

'NO WAY! What were they saying?'

This was the perfect opportunity to get some inside info on my competitors. Mr Wilson suddenly looked awkward.

'Not much . . .' he faded off, looking down and fiddling with a pen, the way he always did when he was nervous.

'Why won't you tell me what they were saying?' I asked quietly. The only reason I could come up with was that he didn't want to share inside information with me, so that he had an unfair advantage in the interview. And though I knew he wanted the job, it still – albeit irrationally – made me feel quite disappointed and hurt. I would have shared secret info with him, had I known any. 'Are you not telling me because you're worried I'll get the promotion over you?' I knew it sounded bitchy and mean but it was better to be honest and communicate openly rather than stew over these thoughts in my mind.

'What?' Mr Wilson looked genuinely hurt. 'Of course not. I would love it if you got the promotion. I'd be happier if you got it than if I got it.'

'Then why won't you tell me what they said?' I pressed harder.

'Because, Mehreen, it's not important. They were talking a whole load of rubbish.' He seemed reluctant to elaborate but knew I wasn't about to let go. 'Lever was basically saying that there's no way you were going to get the job, and that he felt the only competition was between me and him.'

I fell silent. I don't know which I felt more: embarrassed or furious. Mr Wilson seemed embarrassed too, and guilty for telling me.

'Who cares about him anyway, Mehreen? He's a wasteman. I think you've got the best chance.'

But it was all white noise for me at this point. I couldn't believe Mr Fuckface Lever and his shitty, entitled self thought that because he shouted louder and imposed his views on everyone else, he was more qualified than me for this role. I could not believe that he felt I wasn't even in the running – like I was some sort of joke contender.

'Thank you for telling me,' I said quietly. 'I appreciate it.'

And just then, the bell went and it was time for him to leave.

It took a couple of minutes for the initial shock to wear off, but when it did, it was replaced by a rocket up my arse. If Mr Lever wanted to believe I didn't stand a chance of getting a promotion, that was fine. Because there was no way in HELL I was going to let that job slip out of my fingers now.

I didn't eat lunch. I didn't even piss. I was in school until 7.30 that evening, gathering data, matching each bullet point of the job description to specific examples from my career, preparing a list of initiatives run by other successful schools and basically creating a whole folder of evidence about my own prior success as well as a clear vision of a short-, medium- and long-term plan of how I would improve reading levels across the school using the existing pastoral structure. I pulled a favour from my wonderful friends in the library, asking them at the very last minute to pull off the data of the most borrowed books of that year, which they happily did for me. I grafted, toiled and laboured and the next day, I was ready with my presentation in hand, and my make-up immaculate.

As I walked through the canteen towards the interview room, it was like everything was in slow motion. A sea of Year 7s, who were blocking the way, saw me approach, and parted like I was Moses. I gripped firmly my folder of evidence. People may think that you can't be pretty and clever, but I was determined for things to go my way today.

It's always hard to gauge how well you've performed in an interview, because you don't know what everyone else did in there. But I gave it my all, and as I left Mr Thorne's office and started walking back through the canteen, the adrenaline was wearing off and a splitting migraine was starting to emerge in my head.

'Girl, look at you!' Jackie exclaimed, horrified as she saw the sight of me. 'You need to look after yourself and fatten yourself up!' She thrust a carton of chocolate milk in my hand and then, after a second's pause, gave me a packet of crisps too. 'You all right? Who upset you?'

'I'm just tired, Jackie.' I rested my head on her shoulder. She hugged me and I enjoyed the embrace for a few moments. 'Thank you for this. I love you.'

She playfully ruffled my hair, like I was a child. 'Run along now. This place isn't going to clean itself.'

The evening crawled by, as I stared at my phone, waiting for it to ring. 7 p.m. and I had still heard nothing from the school.

'Anything?' I texted Mr Wilson. He sent some laughing emojis back. 'No, Baig. I'll tell you if I hear anything.'

I rolled my eyes and sighed, and placed my phone down. I was just about to ask my mum for a cup of tea when the house phone rang.

'Colonel Baig?' my dad picked up in his usual manner. (He was never in the army.) 'Oh . . . of course, Sir.' He turned towards me. 'Er, Merrin . . .' he said in his most British accent. 'It's for you.'

My whole family stood still like a freeze-frame. My mum and sister grabbed onto each other's hands, my brother looked up from his phone and my father stood there, arm outstretched with the phone towards me, making elaborate thumbs-up gestures. I took the phone.

'Err . . . hello?' My voice was shaking. If I didn't get the role, it wouldn't just be a win for Mr Lever, but also a massive disappointment for my family who believed that I was the best thing since naan bread.

'I'm calling with some good news, Mayrine,' Mr Thorne's familiar Brummie twang came through the speaker. 'We were very impressed with your interview and we would like to offer you the role of Head of Year. Well done, Mayrine.'

As I thanked Mr Thorne, my whole family burst into applause in the background, my dad shouting, 'Thank you, Sir! You're a star!' That night, I slept like a baby.

Walking into my classroom the next morning, I saw a card and some flowers on my desk waiting for me. They were from Mr Wilson. I smiled and texted him to thank him, and then quickly deleted it and wrote 'Better luck next time, hun', followed by a Mean Girls meme, followed by a link to 'We Are the Champions'.

Humility is overrated, and who says I'd grown up?

10

Sometimes, You Have to Learn When to Let Go

The positives of my promotion were that I had a fancy new title, two extra free periods a week and about £100 more a month in my bank account. The negatives were a whole load of additional pointless duties to get through, I was asked to eat lunch whilst standing in the playground so the 'kids were aware of my presence' and I got to spend way less time in the classroom with my students, which is what I joined the profession to actually do.

Lever's dick seemed to have shrivelled even smaller since losing out on the job, hence he went out of his way to not follow any instruction or direction I gave. As fate would have it, he was placed in my team, so he sat in meetings that I was leading, rolling his eyes and huffing and puffing like he was having a peculiar asthma attack and generally making the whole atmosphere quite unpleasant. I decided to speak with Ms Lewis about the best way to handle the situation, before his negativity spread to anyone else.

When I got to her office, Ms Lewis was sitting on her desk, working on her computer. She noticed me walking in and smiled warmly, 'I was just about to come and see you.'

'If something bad has happened, it wasn't me.' I sat down in the chair opposite her as she chuckled.

'OK . . . Lever.'

She threw her head back and burst out laughing at my wide-eyed expression.

'Is the big man-child causing you problems again?'

I nodded.

'I'm not sure how to deal with him. He doesn't respect me – he doesn't even like me. And . . .' I slumped forward, head in my hands. 'I just don't know how to fix it.'

'Mehreen, it's not your problem to fix. He is the one with the problem, so he has to fix it,' she said. She took my hand in hers. 'Once he realises you're not going to take his nonsense any more, he'll back down. It'll only go on for as long as you let it.'

I nodded reluctantly, unsure whether I was brave enough to confront him directly.

'Ask him for a meeting. Put it in writing so you have evidence. And repeat to him, with dates and phrases, everything he has said to you.' She paused. 'Then watch him run off like a little puppy.'

I laughed at the image and squeezed her hand.

'Thank you,' I said. 'And sorry – for disturbing you. I know you're busy.' As I got up to leave, she didn't let go.

'I actually needed to speak to you,' she said.

'Of course,' I said, and as I sat back down, I saw her face properly for the first time. She had dark circles under her eyes and the gold specks that usually glimmered around her pupils had faded. 'Is everything OK?'

'I'm leaving,' she said. It took me a second to process what she had said.

'Leaving what?'

She smiled, but I'm not sure it reached her eyes.

'Leaving school. I'm retiring.'

I stared at her dumbfounded.

'You'll be fine,' she continued. She let go of my hand and leaned towards her desk drawer, rummaging around before pulling out a little wrapped item. She placed it in front of me. 'I saw this and thought of you.'

I picked it up.

'You're meant to fly, Mehreen. Don't sit on the window ledge and watch the world go by. You need to jump so you can fly.'

I was speechless. Her gentle tap on my hand indicated the end of the meeting and, still thinking about those words, I left. Back in my classroom, I sat on my chair and tried to process everything. I reached for the gift and tried to feel the shape with my fingers, then ripped apart the sparkly wrapping paper. Inside, there was a tiny pink flamingo. I laughed through my tears.

With Ms Lewis gone, my main support system had been taken away from me, and I felt scared and vulnerable for a while, almost like I was a newly qualified teacher again. But life moved on, like it always does, and after a while, a school without Ms Lewis became the new norm. Ms Bitcherson and Ms Kowalski took over Ms Lewis's office, and we all carried on practising the policies she had implemented and applying the strategies that she had endorsed, but without her physically there.

Since becoming Head of Year, my relationship with my students had changed, as I now had to hand out regular punishments and sanctions, including those forwarded by other class teachers, and I went from good cop to bad(ish) cop overnight. A number of students in my year group were now on report to me for things like their behaviour, attendance and punctuality. At the end of each day, they had to bring me their report card that had been signed by all their subject teachers and we would discuss it, either praising their achievements or discussing their targets, and then they would be free to go home.

Ethan was one of the boys who was on report to me for his behaviour and his punctuality, and though his behaviour was improving dramatically, he could still never manage to be on time, and it was ruining his position on the progress ladder – one of my own concoctions which stemmed from the idea that students who are not academically able should still be able to gain some rewards or praise for their effort and work ethic. I thought long and hard about how to motivate him to be on time, and decided that I would have to find out the root cause before I could choose a suitable treatment. I phoned home with Ethan sat next to me, so that he could hear me tell his mum that she needed to wake him up earlier in the mornings for him to catch an earlier bus. Ethan's mum said she always woke him up on time but he would either sneak back into bed, or spend ages styling his hair. She also said that Ethan was feeling low and demotivated because despite his improved behaviour, he had not received any encouragement from any teachers and had only got in trouble due to poor punctuality. With the reason behind his lateness firmly established, the best course of antibiotics seemed to be some positive reinforcement, so I tried physically taking Ethan around to each of his teachers to 'get some feedback on how he was doing', and they all played along, overtly gushing about how much he had improved, which he was very pleased with. It worked for about a week, but it wasn't long before he slipped back into his usual pattern again. Then, one afternoon, when he brought me his report, full of 5s for everything except his punctuality, I decided bribery was the only tactic left to try. I told Ethan that if he was on time every morning and for every lesson for the rest of the half-term, I would buy him Nando's for lunch. I wasn't sure how I was going to pull this off, as it would be unfair to the kids who are always on time, but I decided I would cross that bridge when it came.

You know what they say: the simplest solution is almost always the best. The promise of a Peri nice meal worked wonders and for the following few weeks, each morning and for every lesson, Ethan arrived like clockwork. He would pop into my classroom three times a day, excitedly bursting in, waving his report card in the air – 'Miss! Miss! Look!' – and he would thrust the report card under my nose, waiting for my approval with a massive grin on his face. He didn't care whether I was in the middle of something; he was just so proud of himself. I looked at the miraculous little outcome of the unconventional intervention strategy I had used in front of me and giggled at the thought of Ms Bitcherson's horrified expression when I shared it at the next Teaching and Learning forum.

On my way home in Mr Wilson's car, I told him my plan and how well Ethan was doing.

'You couldn't get him to be on time but now look! Look!' I gloated, waving Ethan's report in the air.

'You can't bribe children with food,' Mr Wilson laughed. 'How you going to keep that up?'

'Don't be a hater,' I jested. 'The boy is doing the best he has ever done in school. He deserves a treat. And anyway, we can't all be lemon and herb like you. Life is about taking risks and following the road less travelled.'

The reference was lost on him, but with yet another small victory under my belt, I made myself comfy under his and my jackets, curled up my legs, and drifted into a beautiful snooze.

A few days later, I was sitting in my free period, ploughing through my emails. Since becoming Head of Year, I now received about 100 emails per minute, mostly from various teachers who were 'just letting me know that someone in my year group had behaved completely inappropriately and they will not be having them back in their lesson'. I rolled my eyes at Ms D'Alessio's most recent email, moaning about yet another irrelevant issue. As I worked my way through reams of what this girl did, what that lad did, one by one, I came across an email with the subject 'Miss Baig!!!!'. It was from Martyna.

I had never been so excited to open a work email. It was pages and pages long, asking how I was, sharing her memories of my lessons and telling me what she was up to now. After missing out on her Oxbridge place, she had moved back to Spain and now was training to be an English teacher. She seemed happy.

I was smiling at my screen, right there in the sun with her, when Aurea came into my classroom. 'Is it a love note from Mr Lover Lover?' she said, winking.

'No! It's an email from Martyna. Do you remember her?' I turned on my projector so she could see the email. 'She's becoming an English teacher!'

'I'm so glad for her. You obviously inspired her. Well done, Baigy. Or should I say . . . Robin Williams.'

With that, Aurea jumped onto my table, heels still on, spread out her arms like in *Titanic*, and started shouting 'Captain, my Captain!'

I was in hysterics by this point.

'Aurea! You're going to hurt yourself! Get back down, you lunatic!'

'Captain! My Captain!' she chanted. 'Come on, Baigy!'

Seizing the day, I jumped onto the table opposite her, balancing precariously on my heels, and joined in with, 'O Captain! My Captain!'

As our recitation became more dramatic, Aurea started doing a sort of surfing motion, and I copied. My belly was aching from laughing too much.

'Watch this!' I said, doing a sort of pelvic-thrust motion. 'Aurea!'

'Ummm . . .' I turned to see why she had quietened down, and, to my utter horror, Mr Thorne was standing in my doorway, looking through the glass. As we both came to a standstill, frozen on the table tops, he left without saying a word.

Eventually, it was Nando's day. As soon as I got in, I logged on to my computer and tried to place Ethan's order (possibly with a cheeky quarter-chicken more for myself) but annoyingly, the website did not allow any orders before 11.30 a.m. I calculated that I would place the order during period three – my next free lesson – so that it would arrive just in time for lunch.

I was only halfway through first period when I received a text from Mr Wilson. I smiled, and inconspicuously unlocked my phone to read the message as the class got on with their work.

'Mr Fieldhouse just got someone to cover my lesson and has taken me out to have a word. Not sure what's going on.'

'What? Why? Tell me ASAP!' I replied.

'Will do xx,' he immediately responded.

I was so confused; it took me a second to try to make sense of what was happening. Taking a teacher out during the middle of their lesson was completely unheard of – most things could wait until after the bell. The only time I had ever seen a teacher removed from class was when I was sent home to go and change into a more appropriate outfit – but that's a whole other story for a whole other day. I tried to brainstorm all the possible reasons why Mr Wilson had been summoned, but I could not come up with any logical explanation. Mr Wilson was never in trouble. He never did anything wrong. He followed the rule book to a T. The only thing I could think of Mr Wilson doing against the rules was . . . me. Could it be that senior leadership found out about Mr Wilson sitting in my classes during his free periods and now he was going to be scolded for it? Could someone have hacked into his phone and read some of the not-so-flattering things I had written about Mr Lever? I felt a deep sense of panic building up inside me. Was I next? I checked the time stamp of his last message – it had only been a couple of minutes, but I didn't have the patience to wait. I sent him a line of question marks and then waited for him to read it. He read the text within a few seconds, and I held my breath waiting for a reply – but none came. He must have been in the middle of his meeting and unable to text. A student asked a question, and I forced myself to respond, writing some sentence starters on the board to keep them busy for a while longer. I checked my phone again . . . nothing. It had been three more minutes.

I told myself I would wait two more minutes, because no bollocking would take much longer than five minutes, and after promptly counting to 120 in my head, I sent another line of question marks. Mr Wilson came online, read the question marks, and didn't reply. I was starting to feel irritated – if he could check his phone, he could send back a simple word or two like 'fired' or 'nothing bad' to prepare me for the worst or put my mind at rest.

The lesson ended and Mr Wilson still hadn't texted me back, and my panic turned into dread. This was completely out of character for him – there was no way the meeting could have gone on for this long – and my paranoia had started working overtime. If I were to get fired for my relationship, what would I tell my family? Even the shrill sound of the bell was unable to disrupt the series of alarming scenarios forming in my mind, and as I dismissed the class, I checked my phone again. He was still online.

'Please tell me what is going on???? You're really scaring me,' I typed frantically.

Finally, Mr Wilson was typing. I could feel my heart beating in my chest. He was typing for what seemed like ages, typing and then stopping, and my new class had already started to pour in when the response finally came through. It just said, 'It's not good news, babe.' What kind of vague, ominous, pointless reply was that?

'If this is some sort of sick joke, it's not fucking funny,' I replied. He didn't respond.

Teaching that lesson was so difficult, not only because I was furious at Mr Wilson's lack of communication, but because now I feared it was something to do with me. I could barely keep my hands from shaking. I set the class up on some silent work again, and sat in my chair, waiting for break-time, so I could go and find Mr Wilson and finally unearth what was bloody going on.

About fifteen minutes before the end of the lesson, however, a notice popped up on my computer screen, asking all staff members to report to the staffroom at break-time to discuss some sort of emergency. It took me a minute to recall the last time we were herded together in this way. Ofsted? Another visit from that educational disease was the last thing I needed right now. My immediate thought was that I would take the rest of the week off and I instantly started plotting where I could hide my piles of unmarked exercise books. I don't know why Mr Wilson was being so dramatic and secretive if all this drama was merely about Ofsted coming. The picture was still quite fuzzy because I wasn't sure why Mr Wilson was informed before the rest of us and why we were being subjected to another inspection so soon – but these were minor details, and would soon be resolved. I felt relieved and taught the rest of the lesson in a much better mood, giving more attention to my students, feeling like a weight had been lifted off my shoulders and, once the kids had been dismissed, made my way downstairs to receive the news.

In the staffroom, the teachers all looked how I felt: anxious and curious. I sat next to Aurea and we both held each other's hands as we watched groups of teachers fill up the room, waiting for the briefing to begin. Mr Wilson arrived after everyone else. Usually, he would immediately look around for me, and give me a smile when he spotted my face, but today, he didn't. I tried to catch his eye, shuffling loudly in my seat, coughing, trying to grab his attention, but even as he glanced towards me, he quickly looked away again. Was he avoiding me? I looked at Aurea, whose expression matched my confusion, but then she shrugged in a 'You're reading too much into it' kind of way, and I shrugged back and rolled my eyes in a 'Boys are so bad at communicating' kind of way.

Mr Thorne came to the front and cleared his throat. Near him, Mr Wilson had positioned himself so that I could only see the side of his face – and I knew he could feel me looking at him, but he looked down at the floor. I could have sworn his eyes were red.

'Thank you all for making your way down at such short notice,' Mr Thorne began, 'and apologies for interrupting your lessons, for those of you who were teaching. I know it's not a nice message to receive.' The room was silent in anticipation, and Aurea squeezed my hand. 'Umm, yes,' Mr Thorne cleared his throat again. 'The reason why we have called you down here is to inform you of an incident that took place this morning. It was an incident involving a boy in Year 8 called Ethan Castillo.'

I frowned and looked over to Mr Wilson again, but he was still looking down. I turned to Aurea and she matched my total expression of bewilderment.

'Yes . . . Ethan was on his way to school this morning, when he unfortunately got into an accident.' There were some gasps around the room, and one that escaped my own mouth. Ethan had been in an accident. It must have been serious to necessitate a whole staff meeting. I silently prayed that his injuries were minor and he would be OK.

'Ethan was running for the bus in the morning, when he was unfortunately hit by the bus.' He paused. 'I'm afraid to say, Ethan was pronounced dead at the scene.'

As gasps and shocked screams erupted around me, I freed my hand from Aurea's grip and it flew to my mouth. I felt like I had been punched in my stomach. I felt sick. As a solitary tear poured down my cheek, I turned to look at Mr Wilson. His red eyes looked back at me, apologetic, devastated.

Fifteen minutes after being told, I had to stand in front of a class and inform them of the news. Not only did I have to hide my own tears but had to wipe theirs. I had to stifle my own grief and help them cope with theirs. The moment they all left my class, I locked myself in my classroom, turned the lights off and cried and cried and cried.

I sat with Aurea and Holly at the end of the day, slowly sipping my cup of tea, letting the warmth soothe my throat that felt like it was swollen by now. We had all taken our shoes off and were spread around my classroom. Aurea was lying on my bean bag and Holly had a tissue in her hand that she was slowly tearing to shreds, bit by bit.

'I don't know how people ever get over death,' I said, looking down into my cup. I moved it around and watched the brown liquid swish from side to side.

'I don't think you ever do,' Holly said quietly. The air in the room felt heavy. No one tried to lighten it. 'It's weird how you wake up in the morning and just have no idea what the day is going to bring.'

I rubbed my hands around the warm surface of the cup, thinking about what she had said. Life is unpredictable anyway, but teaching is one endless list of unpredictable moments. In one minute, your whole world can come crashing down. When you are so close to such a large number of people, the chances of experiencing human suffering exponentially increase. Tragedy can come out of nowhere, unexpectedly, and it usually did.

That night, I got home with swollen eyes and smeared make-up, and as I sobbed through the story to my mum, I held on to her tightly, whilst she comforted me. Yet even to her, I couldn't bring myself to say my worst fears aloud – I couldn't ask her whether I was to blame. So what if he was late to a lesson? I would have rather had him late every day just to have him back.

I've seen death. I've been to funerals with mothers mourning. I've seen grieving families utterly devastated by the loss of their loved ones. I thought I was signing up to teach English and inspire young people – to bring them joy and hope and light – but this journey took me to the darkest places and didn't give me any time to find my way out. They say time is a healer, and maybe this pain too would have passed, but this time, it had become too hard, day after day, to just keep going. This time, I wasn't sure I could. I wasn't sure if I wanted to.

I thought about all the times when my colleagues came to the very brink of their patience and talked about leaving the profession – all the times we discussed what other routes they could take, what they could retrain to be, all the times they thought about giving it all up. In my case, I finally did.

Not long after Ethan's death, I decided it was time to hang up my gloves. I didn't tell anyone from school – not my friends and not Mr Wilson – because I knew that would have only made the decision so much harder. I typed out my resignation letter and visited Mr Thorne's office for the last time to hand it in. I told the same man who had heard me and my family's joyous celebration when he offered me the role only a decade ago that I was so grateful for the opportunity, but in the end, the burden was too much.

I was expected to work more hours than there were in the day. I was expected to be outstanding at all times, I could never be just adequate or surviving. I was expected to make decisions that, in truth, no twenty-two-year-old is really qualified to make about someone else's child. Of course, I can still see the incredible value of teaching, but part of growing up is learning when it's time to call it a day and to understand when to let go of something that's no longer a positive force in your life. It's accepting that the struggles outweigh the good and reconciling yourself with the fact that things don't always work out. Change is scary – but sometimes shit happens and you've got to jump off that window ledge before you can fly.

And I was ready to fly.

Epilogue

Letting go of something you once loved and something that was so deeply embedded within your life is difficult. Every day, I wonder if I should have stayed. I wonder if I sold out. I wonder if I should go back. I like to compare teaching to childbirth: as soon as I left the profession, I only remembered the amazing moments and forgot about all the pain. I taught girls who went on to become English teachers, kids who got scholarships into the top schools of the country and boys who became professional footballers – and I can honestly say there is no feeling that compares to that satisfaction.

But as time moves on, the more I understand the importance of carrying the lessons I've learned from the past and moving towards my future. At the time, every second we invested in those kids mattered. The effort we put in and what we achieved was immeasurable. But you can't live in the past or stand still. Today is a new day.

The last time I went back to visit my old school, there was a new lady at the reception who didn't recognise me and requested that I sign in as a visitor. I placed the sticker on my blouse, somewhat affronted (irrational, I know), and sat near the entrance, waiting for Mr Wilson to come and pick me up. He took me around a new one-way system and pointed out the refurbished canteen and the new isolation rooms, until we finally reached the staircase.

The English corridor was still decorated with displays of past students who had achieved grade 9s in their GCSEs and had the same 'Poet-tree' pasted on the wall next to my old classroom. They were using the same roots and branches that I had helped to put up, except with new leaves and poems. Kinsella Corner had been renamed, and the inside of the room was less pink and less cluttered. The same walls that had seen and heard some of my deepest, darkest secrets had now been coated in glossy, new, white paint. None of this was hugely surprising – but still gave me a really weird feeling in my chest. There's something really bizarre about going into a place you feel really territorial about but the remnants of you have gone. The only way I can describe it is that it felt like I was having an out-of-body experience – like I was Dev Patel in *Lion*, able to recognise every path and street, yet unsure of whether this was really once the world I inhabited. That place saw some of my darkest moments and was also where I felt the most fulfilled, and I couldn't figure out whether coming back made me feel sad at being reminded of what I had left behind or grateful for the experiences and memories I had made here – a bit of both, I guess.

I'll always miss the kids. I'll miss their energy. I'll miss being in between the hurricane of their madness, their humour, their drama. I'll miss their unfiltered honesty, their uninhibited transparency, their simplicities and their complexities. I'll miss the way we were all on a journey together to make our lives and the world a better place, one small step at a time. But if I were to return to the school to teach now, it wouldn't be the same. There would be no Ms Lewis to protect and nurture me, no youthful optimism and rose-tinted glasses, and no Aurea and Holly, because they both left teaching to pursue other avenues shortly after I left.

When I hear of teachers leaving the profession, it is always sad because it shows another individual who had the desire to make a difference but ended up walking away. None of us joined teaching for the fame or the money or the glory. We joined because we genuinely cared about those kids and their futures. We joined because we wanted to make a differ-ence. But the profession failed to retain us. What has the potential to be the best, most rewarding, most stimulating job in the world has been utterly ruined by policies and procedures that don't even have the students at the centre of them.

When I look back at my twenties, I genuinely don't know where the years went. Wishing away the weeks and waiting for the next half-term, I guess. When I speak to some of my ex-students who are in their twenties now – older than I was when I used to teach them – I realise how I was little more than a child myself, thrown into the deep end with no armbands or float. I turned thirty with no kids of my own because I devoted every living second to looking after other people's children – yet I have no regrets. I cherish every memory – the good, the bad and the ugly. But when I think about that bright-eyed, bouncy-haired, twenty-one-year-old girl, bursting with enthusiasm, oblivious to any real tra-gedy, I hardly recognise her now.

It took me a good year and a half after leaving teaching just to catch up on sleep and leftover tiredness, and the same amount of time for the daily migraines to ease off, but they eventually did. Teaching was exhilarating and fulfilling but also relentless and unhealthy – and it got to the point where the equilibrium was just not balanced any more. I don't know how much longer my body could have physically continued with the level of stress I was putting it under every single day. By leaving, I could give more time to myself, and to those I loved, and in the long run, I recognised that I only had one shot at a fleeting life, and I had to learn to live it for myself.

Mr Wilson was promoted shortly after I left and is now a part of senior management – a job, as I regularly like to remind him, that would have been mine had I stayed. But perhaps me leaving gave him the space and the time and the freedom to be able to concentrate on his own development and soar without having to always be my anchor. That distance meant we also had the opportunity to upgrade from chicken wings in a classroom to a sit-down feast in Nando's. He kept me up to date with any latest news or gossip, telling me of the 'new Mehreen' who had joined the school – a newly qualified teacher with killer heels, a face full of make-up and a specially curated wardrobe that only a new teacher would have the energy to bother with. The boys giggled and pretended to faint as she walked down the corridor and the PE teachers paid regular visits to her classroom. I told him he must be having a laugh – there was only one Mehreen Baig – but it was clear that even she was replaceable.

You can't go into teaching and think of it as a job. It's not just work, or a 9–5 where you go to pay your bills – it's a vocation. It requires energy, heart and passion. I often hear schools say they're looking to specifically recruit Oxbridge and PhD graduates, and this elitist attitude disregards all the other skills a teacher brings to the table – skills which books can't teach you. It's like they think academia is airborne – but it doesn't work that way. In fact, in all my experience, it is usually the opposite. I have seen numerous Oxbridge grads over the years not being able to survive a year in teaching because the children ate them alive. I have also seen students fail in subjects where a posh git would drone on about university-level theory that wasn't accessible nor relevant to them in Year 8. You can have all the knowledge in the world but it's utterly pointless if you can't deliver and impart that knowledge to the children, if you can't manage their behaviour, if you can't engage them. And once you have lost them, you have really lost them. Teaching is so much more than just the intellectual stuff, and it takes a whole other level of specimen to stay in it for the long haul. Knowing the layers and complexities that the role entails, and the dedication and stamina it requires, and the lack of reward, acknowledgement or praise given in return, my respect for teachers who manage to last is higher than ever before.

In 2020, when education was thrust into the national headlines and home-schooling first began, suddenly everyone was an expert on teaching. While teachers had to evolve, adapt and desperately try to familiarise themselves with new learning platforms and a completely transformative way of teaching digitally, they also had to deal with a barrage of opinions from parents who were now in their virtual classrooms, monitoring the lessons. And if this wasn't enough, they were also subject to a flood of national attacks on social media from people who had absolutely nothing to do with education. I was shocked at how much judgement came from so little understanding.

Initially, teachers finally got some of the credit and recognition they deserved. Billy's mum realised that perhaps he wasn't the little angel she always thought he was, and Cathy's dad discovered she was not, in fact, a child genius. But as the year came to an end and it dawned on people that their free mixing at Christmas might have caused a delay in schools reopening, they were furious at teachers. It was utterly unfathomable why teachers would not jump at the idea of cramming themselves once again into a poorly ventilated classroom for hours on end with thirty miniature pathogens whose idea of 'social distancing' was to only try and lick each other's faces three times an hour instead of seven.

Parents who previously didn't think twice about taking their kids off school for an early, cheap holiday and handed their kids an iPad every day rather than ever reading them a book became advocates for the importance of education. The same government that had previously slashed millions of pounds from youth services and another billion from schools was suddenly overwhelmingly concerned about student mental health. Whilst professionals around the country were preparing to continue doing Zoom meetings with no pants on until it was safe to start socialising again, it was suggested – and accepted – that teachers would add sticking swabs up their students' possibly infected throats and noses to their list of never-ending duties.

In Nick Carraway's words, the teachers still 'beat on . . . boats against the current' and although my direction slightly altered in the wind, I remain on that sea with

them. I may have missed out on the joys of online learning during the pandemic, but I did still share the dread
and anxiety as I watched my family and colleagues being
sent like lambs to the slaughter – and I must admit, I may
have got into a few Twitter spats. My brother was incredibly high risk, yet had to go into work every day, and as
teachers and students in his school were sent home daily
to quarantine after testing positive for Covid-19, my
family spent the entire year of 2020 in perpetual fear. It
was like watching Wilfred Owen return to the trenches
with the foresight of knowing what could happen to him
but unable to do anything to stop it.

My heart broke for my family, friends and colleagues who
I knew had spent the year slogging in their homes and in
classrooms, creating home-learning materials, teaching
online lessons, delivering food parcels and laptops to disadvantaged students – sometimes purchased from their own
money – yet there was no Thursday clap for them. All they
received in return was a torrent of abuse and criticism.

The pandemic made the disparities in education even
more exposed. Whilst my friend's private-school students
were getting live, timetabled online lessons every day, my
kids didn't have laptops or reliable broadband, or any way to
access any form of education for a year. The government
had £200,000 to replace their unwanted John Lewis furni-
ture, and another £200 million for a memorial yacht, but
not enough money to provide students with education and
food.

The residual effect of the pandemic is going to have a lasting impact on teacher and student welfare: kids are not just
behind on academic progress but their mental health is
worse than ever before – not just because thousands of

children were locked indoors in cramped, overcrowded council flats with no fancy gardens for the best part of a year, but also because many of them spent that year confined in severely unsafe and abusive situations. And all of this will have a knock-on effect on the future of those students, who will also get lower centre-assessed grades than their private-school counterparts, and who will not gain the qualifications necessary for the next step, exacerbating the inequality that was already rife.

At twenty-one, I couldn't have cared less about politics. I cared about individual stories and individual people, but I didn't have an understanding or insight about society at large. But after witnessing the way some children have been left at the bottom rung of the ladder for ten years, constantly being affected by choices made by everyone but them, it is difficult, if not impossible, to avoid looking beyond the single story.

I will always stand in solidarity with teachers. I will always champion young people and advocate for a more equal society. I will always be able to do eight people's work through my superpower ability of multitasking. Teaching has definitely served its purpose. And everything I learned in that school shaped, and will continue to shape, my life.

Even when teachers leave the profession, they still exist. They still live on in the kids they taught whose lives they changed. Their words, their values, their lessons are passed down generation after generation. They still matter.

Teaching was my first job, and it will always hold a really special place in my heart. It's like your first relationship – you go into it with no experience, with no walls or guard up, just open and vulnerable and exposed and ready and willing to take all the hits. And of course I took hits. But with each injury, I repaired stronger, a little bit thicker and was never quite the same.

The only thing that didn't repair was the thrush.

Because I'm still stressed and still working way too hard in the hope of, one day, saving the world.

Acknowledgements

I'm sure most authors will say writing a book is a 'dream come true', but I don't really know how else to put it. Even as I write this, it doesn't quite feel real.

It's been a bloody journey to get to this point, I tell ya. Thirty-one years of pure hustle. I used to write stories with those little, blue pens you got for free from Argos in the corner of my very crowded, very noisy house, and now I'm going to be a published author. Do you know how wild that is?

None of this would have been possible without the love, support and guidance of the people around me – the people who have played a vital role in this process and in my life.

I'd firstly like to thank my colleagues and my friends at my school, without whom this book wouldn't exist, because I would have no stories to tell. The headteacher gave me a job despite my terrible naivety because he must have seen something in me that, at that point, I couldn't even see in myself. I feel so grateful that the beginning of my adult life was spent in such an incredible place. The second I stepped foot in that building, I knew that was where I belonged. My department and my friends, especially Ordella, Sophie and

Maarya, thank you for making such special memories with me. Sophie, thank you for allowing and trusting me to share your story. It means so much to me.

Odette, you have helped me through every stage of my journey – not just when writing the book, but so much before that. You have allowed me to endlessly pick your brain and shared your incomparable intelligence with me. You have given me your time and your support like a true sister. I hope you know that I will always be here to do the same for you.

Equally, I'd like to thank the students who I taught. Looking after them, teaching them and learning from them was an absolute honour. I cherish the time we spent together.

I'd also like to thank Usama, who has been my lifeline since university. A few years ago, he spent endless hours helping me create my first blogging website. This was the platform where I first shared my writing with the public. I didn't have enough money to pay him anything and he never expected anything in return. He simply helped me out of the goodness of his heart, and I will never forget it. Little did we know at the time, that website would go on to change my life forever. I continue to phone him every week, usually panicking and in tears because I've accidentally deleted my book or something, and he always helps me to retrieve it, even though he moans more than he used to. He is a genius, but more than that, a fantastic friend.

Another godsend for me in the last few years has been Samir Ahmed at Media Hive (Sammy). When I joined this industry, I knew no one. I had no real friends. I had no one I could really trust. And that can be so difficult. If it wasn't for Samir, I really don't know what I would have done. His friendship has been utterly invaluable for me. There has not been a single thing I have needed since I left teaching that

Sammy hasn't gone out of his way to help me with. He is busy enough as it is with his own work, and yet he has put hours aside every single day to help sort my life out. When I sent him a draft of my book to read over, he printed the whole thing out (that's a lot of paper and ink) and physically wrote pages and pages of comments and feedback. Thank you, Sammy, for everything.

Tracey and Russell at KBJ Management, thank you for helping me navigate a world that was so new to me and for helping this book turn from an idea into a reality. This is, by far, the most exciting project of my life and I love you for your guidance and your belief in me.

Jon Wood, thank you for all your help with putting together my proposal. You didn't have to help me – but you did, and it made all the difference.

Dan Hills, thank you for being the most wonderful friend over the last few months and for coming down all the way from Brighton to help me. I appreciate you so much.

Thank you to Bobby Seagull and all my other brilliant friends who answered my random phone calls when I was stuck or needed to double-check if something I had written was funny or not. Thank you for picking up the phone.

Lauren, Jaimie and Toni, thank you for taking the time out to read chapters of my book and give me feedback. You could have just not replied to my text. I still can't believe you took out so much time for me. Thank you so much.

Paul Jones (Pauly) you were the best dial-a-word service. If you were genuinely a company, you would be bankrupt, but thank you for always trying your best to help me, and always with that delightful smile on your face.

I can honestly say, I could not have wished for a better publisher. Working with Hodder Studio has been an absolute dream. Thank you to everyone who has read the book at every stage and been so supportive and helpful and understanding and encouraging – in particular Izzy Everington and Kwaku Osei-Afrifa, thank you for checking over my book and putting so much effort into it. And Harriet Poland – I genuinely believe it's fate I ended up with you as my editor. Thank you for believing in me and my idea from our very first conversation, for listening to and paying attention to every single thought and worry I had and most of all, thank you for letting the book be uncompromisingly mine. You are everything I wanted in an editor and more, and I will forever appreciate your kindness and respect for me, my words, my perspective and my story.

Neil, Jonny and Chris at Insanity, I realised soon after meeting you that writing a book is not all roses, and when shit hit the fan, you really stepped up to support me. You made me feel so safe and protected, during an incredibly overwhelming and scary time, and I can't tell you how much that meant to me.

Joey (Jojo), thank you for spending so much time reading and editing chapters with me, when you could have been partying or doing anything more fun. Even though you read really slowly, you made the whole process so much more enjoyable and you honestly did help to make the book what it is. The bits you helped me with are my favourite.

James, you never helped me with my book, but as you'll see, you are a key part of my story, and a key part of my life. I know the three months I was writing this book were not easy – I was absent, physically and mentally. Your patience with me deserves a medal. Thank you for putting up with me on my worst days and my worst moments. You were the best thing to come out of the last decade.

Fil, the draft of this book is still in your inbox. Have you opened it yet? I don't think so. Maybe you won't even read this book, because you'd rather watch *Eastenders*, so I'll have to read this bit out to you when you're at my house next. I want you to know that you are the bestest friend any human being could ask for. You are more than a friend – you are a part of my soul. If it wasn't for you, I wouldn't even be alive. So even though you were utterly useless in this book writing process, thank you for being my life support machine.

And to my family – you are the wildest, craziest, loudest, loveliest family in the world, and I thank God every day that I have you.

Ali, my brother, thank you for buying me my first computer and my first phone and for making sure I never went without, no matter what you had to sacrifice. Even though I'm not your favourite sister, I love you so much and appreciate everything you have done – and continue to do – for me.

Donna, you are the greatest addition to the family I could have ever asked for. Your brutal honesty is what every girl needs and your unwavering strength inspires me every day.

Amelia and Zach, thank you for bringing a smile to my face every single morning. Your little faces light up my life.

Dad, you are the one who taught me to be unapologetically me and taught me to be true to myself. My humour, imagination and honesty are all from you.

Mum, you are my world. You did everything single-handedly while I was locked in a room for weeks writing this book, and you never moaned or complained. You brought tea up to my room, fed me and loved me. You are my everything – you are my strength and my motivation – and all I want in this world is to see you smile. I hope you are proud of me, even though there are loads of rude words in this book. Log kya kaheinge?

Finally, my sister, Ambreen. I don't think saying thank you is enough. I wanted to write pages and pages for you, but nothing I say will ever express my gratitude towards you. You have taught me everything I know. If I can read or write or teach, it is all because of you. This book only exists because you sat with me, every single day and every single night, past your bedtime, and checked over every single word with me. It was like my dissertation but on steroids. You are the most thoughtful, helpful, selfless, beautiful, clever, competent, reliable, incredible person to walk this earth, and I am in awe of you and the sunshine you bring to this world every single day. The whole world can turn their backs on me, but it won't matter because I have you, and you are all I need and more. You are a blessing. It is nowhere near enough, but thank you for being my sister.

Sorry I ruined everyone's lives for twelve weeks, boring everyone to death, talking about nothing else but the book, infiltrating the group chat with book updates, insisting on silence in the house and refusing to leave the bedroom under any circumstance. Thank you for not disowning me. I am so blessed to have all of you.

I hope you enjoy the final product, that you have all helped to create.